KEY TO HARDINESS ZONES

D0008463

'even
based on
minimum
ded for the
The zone
ying the
indicate
rneir lower limits of winter cold
hardiness. Extreme summer
heat and humidity also play a
part in a plant's adaptability;
many plants hardy in colder
zones grow poorly in warmer,
wetter ones.

1	BELOW −50°F	BELOW −46°C
2	−50° TO −40°F	−46° TO −40°C
3	−40° TO −30°F	−40° TO −34°C
4	−30° TO −20°F	−34° TO −29°C
5	−20° TO −10°F	−29° TO −23°C
6	−10° TO 0°F	−23° TO −18°C
7	0° TO 10°F	−18° TO −12°C
8	10° TO 20°F	−12° TO −7°C
9	20° TO 30°F	−7° TO −1°C
10	30° TO 40°F	−1° TO 4°C
11	ABOVE 40°F	ABOVE 4°C

EYEWITNESS
GARDEN HANDBOOKS
ROSES

EYEWITNESS
GARDEN HANDBOOKS
ROSES

DK

A DK PUBLISHING BOOK

Produced for Dorling Kindersley by PAGE One
Cairn House, Elgiva Lane, Chesham, Buckinghamshire

EDITOR Helen Parker
DESIGNER Bob Gordon
MANAGING EDITOR Francis Ritter
MANAGING ART EDITOR Derek Coombes
PRODUCTION Adrian Gathercole
PICTURE RESEARCH Sharon Southren

First American Edition 1996
2 4 6 8 10 9 7 5 3

Published in the United States by
DK Publishing, Inc., 95 Madison Avenue, New York, NY 10016

Visit us on the World Wide Web at
http://www.dk.com

Published in the US by DK Publishing, Inc.
Distributed by Houghton Mifflin Company, Boston.

Library of Congress Cagaloging-in-Publication Data

Roses. — 1st ed.
p. cm. — (Eyewitness garden handbooks)
Includes index.
ISBN 0-7894-0607-1
1. Rose cuture. 2. Roses—Pictorial works. I. Series.
SB411.R659917 1996
635.9'33372—dc20   95-43904
                                                   CIP

Color reproduction by Colourscan, Singapore
Printed and bound in Singabpore by Star Standard Industries

Contents

Contributors
Peter Harkness
Consultant

Linden Hawthorne
Writer

HOW TO USE THIS BOOK

THIS BOOK PROVIDES the ideal quick reference guide to selecting and identifying roses for the garden.

The introductory section **Roses in the Garden** gives useful advice on choosing a suitable rose for a particular site or purpose: a modern shrub for a formal border; a vigorous climber to conceal an ugly expanse of wall; a low-growing ground-cover rose to cascade over a terrace; or a flower-laden miniature to grow in a container on a patio.

To choose or identify a particular rose, turn to the **Catalog of Garden Roses,** where each full-color photograph is accompanied by a clear, concise plant description. Helpful tips on use and any special pruning or training requirements are also to be found under each plant entry, as well as parentage, origin and date, and any synonyms.

The entries are grouped into six main sections according to type and use: **modern bush, modern shrub, old garden and species, ground-cover, patio and miniature,** and **climbers and ramblers**. To make it easier to select roses of a preferred color, each section is organized by color (see the color wheel below).

For general information on selecting and growing roses, pruning and training, routine care, and propagation turn to the **Guide to Rose Care.**

THE SYMBOLS

The symbols below are used in the **Catalog of Roses** to indicate, at a glance, the preferred growing conditions and hardiness. Most roses are hardy to a minimum of 5°F (-15°C) and will do best if placed in a sunny position in well-drained soil.

☼ Prefers full sun   ◊ Prefers well-drained soil

☼ Prefers partial shade   ◖ Prefers moist soil

☀ Tolerates full shade   ● Prefers wet soil

pH Needs acid soil

Hardiness
The range of winter temperatures that each plant is able to withstand is shown by the USDA plant hardiness zone numbers that are given in each entry. The temperature ranges for each zone are shown on the endpaper map in this book.

Many modern roses require winter protection in much of North America. Generally, the colder the winter, the more protection is required; some roses are best grown as annuals in very cold areas.

Protection systems range from a light covering of straw to burying the entire plant in a deep trench. Consult local experts for detailed advice.

At the end of the book, useful terms are clearly explained in the two-page glossary, and a comprehensive index of every rose and its synonyms gives easy access to the book by plant name.

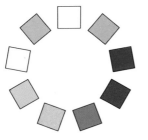

The color wheel
All the roses featured in the book are grouped according to the color of their flowers. They are always arranged in the same order, indicated by the color wheel (left), from white through reds and blues, to yellows and oranges.

HOW TO USE THE CATALOG OF ROSES

The rose's *common* or *popular* name(s) (if any) appears here.

The rose's *classification group* appears here (see page 14). This information will help you know how to prune and care for your rose.

TIPS
Helpful information on use and cultivation of each rose, including notes on pruning and training where details are specific to the entry. For general advice on cultivation turn to the **Guide to Rose Care**.

ORIGIN
For species roses, the origin tells you where the species can be seen in the wild. For cultivars, the breeder and date or the rose's first appearance are given.

The rose's *botanical* or *cultivar name* appears here.

ENTRIES
Each entry begins with a plant description including information on the rose's growing habit, flowers, hips (where relevant), leaves, and blooming period.

PARENTAGE
The parentage of the rose tells you how the cultivar was created.

OTHER NAMES
These are other names under which a rose may be sold or described.

HEADINGS
A running head at the top of each page tells you which section of the book you are in. The book is divided into six main sections (see previous page).

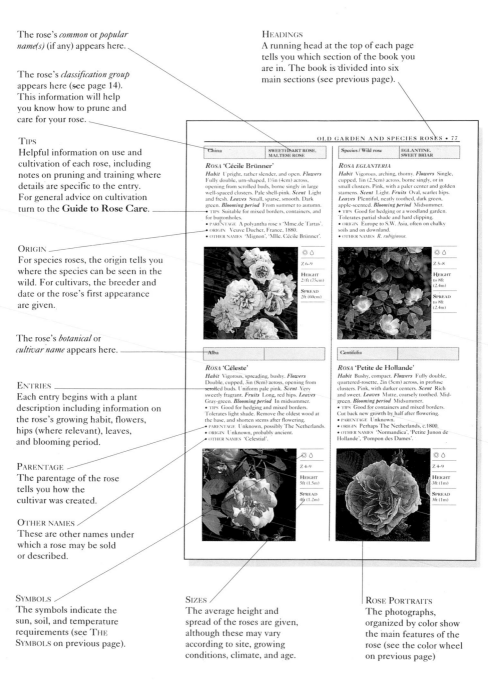

OLD GARDEN AND SPECIES ROSES • 77

China	SWEETHEART ROSE, MALTESE ROSE

ROSA **'Cécile Brünner'**
Habit Upright, rather slender, and open. **Flowers** Fully double, urn-shaped, 1½in (4cm) across, opening from scrolled buds, borne singly in large well-spaced clusters. Pale shell-pink. **Scent** Light and fresh. **Leaves** Small, sparse, smooth. Dark green. **Blooming period** From summer to autumn.
• TIPS Suitable for mixed borders, containers, and for buttonholes.
• PARENTAGE A polyantha rose x 'Mme.de Tartas'.
• ORIGIN Veuve Ducher, France, 1880.
• OTHER NAMES 'Mignon', 'Mlle. Cécile Brünner'.

☼ ◊
Z 6–9
HEIGHT 2½ft (75cm)
SPREAD 2ft (60cm)

Species / Wild rose	EGLANTINE, SWEET BRIAR

ROSA EGLANTERIA
Habit Vigorous, arching, thorny. **Flowers** Single, cupped, 1in (2.5cm) across, borne singly, or in small clusters. Pink, with a paler center and golden stamens. **Scent** Light. **Fruits** Oval, scarlet hips. **Leaves** Plentiful, neatly toothed, dark green, apple-scented. **Blooming period** Midsummer.
• TIPS Good for hedging or a woodland garden. Tolerates partial shade and hard clipping.
• ORIGIN Europe to S.W. Asia, often on chalky soils and on downland.
• OTHER NAMES *R. rubiginosa*.

☼ ◊
Z 5–8
HEIGHT to 8ft (2.4m)
SPREAD to 8ft (2.4m)

Alba	

ROSA **'Céleste'**
Habit Vigorous, spreading, bushy. **Flowers** Double, cupped, 3in (8cm) across, opening from scrolled buds. Uniform pale pink. **Scent** Very sweetly fragrant. **Fruits** Long, red hips. **Leaves** Gray-green. **Blooming period** In midsummer.
• TIPS Tolerates light shade. Remove the oldest wood at the base, and shorten stems after flowering.
• PARENTAGE Unknown, possibly The Netherlands.
• ORIGIN Unknown, probably ancient.
• OTHER NAMES 'Celestial'.

☼ ◊
Z 4–9
HEIGHT 5ft (1.5m)
SPREAD 4ft (1.2m)

Centifolia	

ROSA **'Petite de Hollande'**
Habit Bushy, compact. **Flowers** Fully double, quartered-rosette, 2in (5cm) across, in profuse clusters. Pink, with darker centers. **Scent** Rich and sweet. **Leaves** Matte, coarsely toothed. Mid-green. **Blooming period** Midsummer.
• TIPS Good for containers and mixed borders. Cut back new growth by half after flowering.
• PARENTAGE Unknown.
• ORIGIN Perhaps The Netherlands, c.1800.
• OTHER NAMES 'Normandica', 'Petite Junon de Hollande', 'Pompon des Dames'.

☼ ◊
Z 4–9
HEIGHT 3ft (1m)
SPREAD 3ft (1m)

SYMBOLS
The symbols indicate the sun, soil, and temperature requirements (see THE SYMBOLS on previous page).

SIZES
The average height and spread of the roses are given, although these may vary according to site, growing conditions, climate, and age.

ROSE PORTRAITS
The photographs, organized by color show the main features of the rose (see the color wheel on previous page)

ROSES IN THE GARDEN

ROSES HAVE BEEN LOVED and revered since pre-Roman times for the extraordinary fragrance and beauty of their blooms. The genus *Rosa* offers the gardener an unrivaled diversity of flower shape, color, and scent, ranging from the elegant simplicity of a species rose to the soft pastel colors and intense perfumes of the old garden roses, or the jewel-like brilliance of the modern hybrids. Few plants are so varied as the rose in its growth habit, height, foliage and form. Roses can be used to create any style or mood of planting, from restrained classicism to luxuriant informality. They can be selected to suit almost any situation in the garden, whether using miniature or patio roses in window boxes or pots in a courtyard, or a huge rambler to clothe an old tree with foaming profusion in summer. They can be grown alone as specimens, used as screens or hedging, massed in formal borders, or used to enhance the charm and abundance of a mixed border. Most roses are long-lived, so it is important at the outset to choose the right plant for a particular site.

Choosing roses
The vast number of rose cultivars available can make choice bewildering, and the list is added to annually. Before making a final choice, visit established gardens to see as many different types of rose as possible growing in a garden situation. Do this over a period of time to assess habit, height and spread, vigor, and resistance to disease. Look for less obvious ornamental virtues such as attractive and plentiful foliage, conspicuous thorns, or brightly colored hips. Take note of flower fragrance and

A well-planned rose garden
A stylish and subtle color theme in which shrub roses blend with perennials to create a mood of restful profusion.

FLOWER SHAPES

Flat *Open, usually single or semi-double, with petals that are almost flat.*

Cupped *Open, single to fully double, with petals curving upward and outward from the center.*

Pointed *Semi-double to fully double, with tight, high-pointed centers, typical of Hybrid Teas.*

Urn-shaped *Semi-double to fully double, flat-topped with curving petals, a classic Hybrid Tea shape.*

Rounded *Double or fully double, with even-sized overlapping petals forming a bowl-shaped outline.*

Rosette *Flattish, double or fully double, with many confused, slightly overlapping petals of uneven size.*

Quartered-rosette *Flattish, double or fully double, with confused, uneven petals arranged in a quartered pattern.*

Pompon *Small, rounded, double, or fully double, with masses of small petals; blooms are usually clustered.*

color and its endurance in strong sun. Observe and research a rose's continuity of flowering. Bear in mind that while most old garden roses bloom only once in profusion in midsummer, many modern ones will continue to bloom throughout summer until the first hard frosts.

Suppliers' catalogs provide an excellent source of information and inspiration. Many local rose societies maintain lists of roses stocked by local and mail-order nurseries. These can prove invaluable in locating suppliers, especially of the more unusual roses.

Flower shapes

The diversity of flower form ranges from the simple, single flowers of a species rose to the elegant high-pointed shape of a Hybrid Tea or the complex rosette form that characterizes many old garden roses. The flower forms shown above indicate shape at the peak of a flower's perfection, often just before fully open. They may be single (4–7 petals), semi-double (8–14 petals), double (15–20 petals), or fully double (over 30 petals).

Fragrance, color, hips, and thorns

Most old garden roses, and some modern roses, possess enchanting perfumes with a hints of musk, honey, lemon, spice, or fresh China tea. Rose scent varies in character and intensity with the age of the flower, the time of day, humidity, and the "nose" of the individual gardener. A good tip is to plant fragrant roses near a window or door, around a patio or path or in a sheltered area where the scent will permeate the still, warm air of a summer evening.

Modern roses embrace nearly every color of the spectrum, except for true blue, and range from soft pastels to bright golden-yellows and vibrant vermilions that are often fast in strong light. The old

Informal style
Here, roses form an informal and fragrant backdrop to herbaceous perennials, with pale spires of delphiniums and soft blue campanulas providing effective contrasts of color and form.

roses possess pure tones from the cleanest of whites through every shade of pink to crimson, violet, and purple, the dark shades often fading gracefully to reveal dusky tints of lavender, magenta, gray, and old rose. Roses co-ordinate well together and with other plants but, in general, it is best to avoid combinations of too many bright colors. The association of vermilion with magenta, for example, will be harsh and discordant to many. Such strong hues are best separated with soft pastels or whites to create a harmonious balance of cool and hot shades.

Foliage also provides ornamental effects, as with the wrinkled brilliant greens of *Rosa rugosa* hybrids, or the soft gray-purples of *R. glauca* and the gray- or blue-tinted greens of *R. alba* and its variants. A number of roses, such as *R. virginiana*, have vivid foliage tints in autumn. In single- and semi-double flowered variants of *R. rugosa*, autumn color is enhanced by the production of large, glossy red hips. Many species roses bear conspicuously attractive hips with a color range from yellow through red to glossy black-purple; those of *R. moyesii* and its hybrids are flask-shaped and brightly colored.

Some roses also bear ornamental thorns, most notably *R. sericea* subsp. *omeiensis*, with triangular thorns that glow ruby-red when backlit by the sun.

Formal rose gardens
The traditional rose garden with formal beds laid out in geometric precision is still a popular means of displaying roses, and many modern cultivars, with their long flowering period, elegant blooms, and strongly upright habit, are especially suited to the classic elegance of formal plantings. These are most successful using roses that have a similar peak flowering period, setting cultivars in

groups of five or six to form regular and substantial blocks of toning color. Open beds look best with cultivars of uniform height, although they may be enhanced by focal plantings with standard roses to give additional height. A rose bed backed by a wall or hedge offers potential for plantings of graduated height, with the lower-growing cultivars at the front.

Informal plantings

The charm of roses may be exploited in a wide range of informal planting designs, particularly when used with herbaceous plants or other shrubs. The variations of stature and habit, chosen from the numerous cultivars of groundcover and miniature roses, through shrub roses to ramblers and climbers, provide plants that are suitable for a diversity of situations. The growth habit of many shrub roses, such as the airy China roses or the lax Damasks, lends itself well to use in a mixed border, adding informal profusion while providing height and structure. On steep sites, terraces can provide a striking setting for roses. A combination of graceful shrub roses on the level tops, with ramblers or ground-cover roses cascading down the face, creates dynamic graduations of height and perspective.

Many roses combine happily with herbaceous underplantings, providing they are shallow-rooting or spaced to permit access to the rose root area for mulching and feeding. Herbaceous plants can highlight the particular beauties of a rose, or provide interest when the rose has finished blooming. Scented plants, such as lavender, violas, catmint, the clove pinks (*Dianthus*), or

Flowers and foliage
The rich, jewel-like colors of the rose blooms are set against an elegant underplanting of herbs with gray-green foliage, all toning beautifully with the soft, neutral buff of gravel.

Ornamental arch
The fragrant and repeat-flowering modern climber, R. 'Bantry Bay' has rich pink, old-fashioned flowers. It has been trained here onto a rustic arch to create a division in the garden and to form an enticing and decorative frame for the view beyond.

rocket (*Hesperis*) add their own perfume to a potpourri of rose scents, as well as providing color and textural contrasts. Taller, midsummer-flowering plants, such as *Campanula lactiflora*, *Lilium regale*, or the foxglove *Digitalis purpurea*, with its upright purple spires, are delightful companions when grown through old garden roses, adding striking contrasts of color, form, and habit. Many roses combine well with gray-leaved plants, such as *Stachys byzantina* or the finely cut artemisias, and especially with aromatic evergreens such as sage (*Salvia officinalis*) and *Santolina chamaecyparissus*, which also lend structure to a border in winter. In spring, interest can be extended with bulbs such as species tulips, delicate narcissus, *Chionodoxa*, and snowdrops (*Galanthus*).

Both shrub and species roses combine well with other shrubs, providing they receive sufficient sun. They can be used to complement earlier flowering shrubs;

for instance those with long, questing branches, such as *R.* 'Complicata', are very effective if allowed to scramble through, and bring life to, dull summer foliage. Scented shrubs, such as *Philadelphus*, prove useful companions since they flower in midsummer, adding their own fragrance to that of the rose.

Climbers and ramblers
Most rambling and climbing roses are vigorous plants, producing an exuberance of bloom in summer. They may be grown as specimens to form decorative features in their own right, used to complement other climbers such as clematis, or planted to scramble through other wall-trained shrubs or even old trees. They are invaluable for clothing arbors, walls, and fences, for disguising unsightly garden buildings, or to lend height to a summer border.

Strictly speaking, ramblers produce long, flexible canes annually from the base, which are cut out after flowering. Climbers have a stiffer, more upright habit of growth, and generally flower on laterals arising from the previous year's wood; they are usually pruned back annually to a permanent woody framework. The distinction has been blurred in some cases by the process of hybridization, but it is important to consider this difference in habit when selecting roses for a particular situation. The flexible shoots of ramblers are easier to train on complex structures such as pergolas, arches, tunnels, or trellises, or to form swags and garlands on a catenary (ropes or chains suspended between rigid uprights). When grown against a wall, they sometimes succumb to mildew as a result of poor air circulation. The stiffer habit of true climbers is better suited to training on a wall, clothing a fence, or for free-standing pillars.

Whether you choose a climber or rambler, however, it is important to select one that will adequately cover, but not outgrow, the intended space. It is also essential that all supports are sufficiently strong to bear the weight of the plant at maturity. Although rustic wooden supports and trellises are often more attractive than metal supports initially, bear in mind that, even if treated, they will eventually rot away at ground level.

Groundcover, miniature and patio roses

These roses, many of which flower throughout summer, have greatly extended the range of situations in which roses can be used. The miniature and patio roses are invaluable in confined spaces, in raised beds, and in a range of containers for decorating patios and other paved areas in the garden. Groundcover roses are ideal for low plantings at the front of a border, in both formal and informal situations, and often give of their best when cascading over a low wall, or when used to clothe a steep bank that is otherwise difficult to plant. Only those of really dense habit provide weed-smothering groundcover, and even these are only effective if the ground is weed-free to start with.

Autumn hips
The large, brilliant scarlet hips of this species rose contrast vividly with the more delicate, attractively gold-margined leaves.

Roses in containers
Miniature roses are ideal for containers. The pale pink flowers shown here, elegantly offset the shape and color of the simple terracotta pot.

ROSE CLASSIFICATION

Roses have been cultivated for hundreds of years, during which time they have been widely hybridized to produce a vast number of shrubs suitable for growing as specimen plants, in the border, as hedges and as climbers for training on walls, pergolas, and pillars. Roses are classified into three main groups:

SPECIES
Species, wild roses and their hybrids Mostly large shrubs or climbers with mainly single flowers in spring or summer, followed by decorative hips in autumn.

OLD GARDEN ROSES
Alba Large, freely branching shrubs with usually gray-green foliage, and clusters of 5–7 flowers in midsummer.
Bourbon Vigorous, open, remontant (repeat-flowering) shrubs with fragrant, double flowers, often in 3s, in summer-autumn.
Centifolia (Provence) Lax, thorny shrubs with arching canes bearing clusters of 1–3 large, fragrant, many-petaled flowers in midsummer.
China Small to medium shrubs of light, airy habit with small, mainly double flowers borne singly or in clusters in summer-autumn.
Damask Lax, graceful shrubs bearing loose clusters of 5–7 very fragrant flowers, mainly in midsummer.

Gallica Dense, upright, shrubs with richly colored, often fragrant flowers, up to 3 to a cluster, in midsummer.
Hybrid Perpetual Vigorous, mostly remontant shrubs with flowers borne singly or in 3s in summer-autumn.
Moss Derived from the centifolias and damasks, and similar in habit and flowering to them, with mossy growth on the stems and calyces.
Noisette Remontant climbers bearing large clusters of up to 9 fragrant flowers in summer-autumn.
Portland Upright, dense, less vigorous but more remontant than bourbons. Flowers in summer-autumn.
Sempervirens Semi-evergreen climbers bearing numerous flowers in late summer.
Tea Remontant shrubs and climbers bearing loose, often fragrant, usually double flowers, singly or in 3s, in summer-autumn.

MODERN GARDEN ROSES
Shrub A diverse group, mostly remontant, ranging from low, mound-forming cultivars to wide-spreading shrubs and giant cluster-flowered bushes.
Hybrid Tea (Large-flowered bush) Upright, remontant shrubs with mostly pointed, often fragrant, double flowers borne singly, or in 3s, in summer-autumn.
Floribunda (Cluster-flowered bush) Upright, remontant shrubs, with

sometimes fragrant, single to fully double flowers, in clusters of 3 to 25, in summer-autumn.

Dwarf cluster-flowered bush (Patio) Similar to floribunda roses, but smaller and neater in habit.
Miniature bush Tiny, remontant counterparts of hybrid tea roses.
Polyantha Tough, compact, remontant shrubs with many small flowers in summer and autumn.
Groundcover Trailing or spreading, mostly remontant roses with small leaves, and clusters of 3–11 small flowers, in summer-autumn.
Climber Climbing roses, sometimes remontant, with long, stiff shoots, and flowers borne singly or in clusters, from late spring to autumn. Includes a small group (e.g. 'Albertine') that are between a climber and rambler in habit.
Rambler Vigorous climbing roses with long, flexible shoots bearing single to fully double blooms in clusters of 3–21, in summer.

CATALOG OF
ROSES

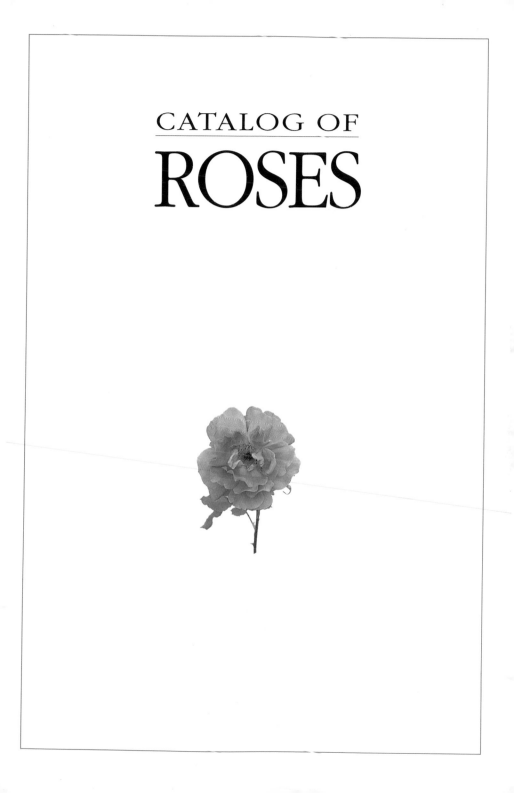

Hybrid Tea (Large-flowered bush)	

ROSA 'Ice Cream'

Habit Dense, upright. **Flowers** Double, rounded, 6in (15cm) across. White, very faintly flushed lemon-yellow. **Scent** Sweet, light, and delicate. **Leaves** Dark green, coppery-red when young. **Blooming period** Summer to autumn.
• TIPS Good for cutting, bedding, and borders. Also useful as a standard.
• PARENTAGE Not disclosed.
• ORIGIN Kordes, Germany, 1992.
• OTHER NAMES 'Korzuri'.

☼ ◊

Z 5–9

HEIGHT
32in (80cm)

SPREAD
28in (70cm)

Hybrid Tea (Large-flowered bush)	

ROSA 'Polar Star'

Habit Vigorous, upright, well-branched, free-flowering. **Flowers** Double, pointed, 5in (12cm) across, on strong stems. **Scent** Light, fresh, and sweet. **Leaves** Rather sparse, but large, glossy. Mid- to dark green. **Blooming period** Summer to autumn.
• TIPS Good for beds, borders, and for cutting and exhibition. Robust and easily grown.
• PARENTAGE Not disclosed.
• ORIGIN Tantau, Germany, 1982.
• OTHER NAMES 'Tanlarpost', 'Polarstern'.

☼ ◊

Z 5–9

HEIGHT
3ft (1m)

SPREAD
28in (70cm)

Floribunda (Cluster-flowered bush)	

ROSA 'Gruss an Aachen'

Habit Bushy, low, upright. **Flowers** Fully double, cupped, 4–5in (10–12cm) across, with silky petals, in clusters. Creamy-white with peachy highlights. **Scent** Soft and sweet. **Leaves** Matte, leathery. Dark green. **Blooming period** Summer to autumn.
• TIPS A tough, reliable rose for bedding, hedging and containers; may be forced under glass. Suitable for mixed borders and informal plantings.
• PARENTAGE 'Frau Karl Druschki' x 'Franz Deegen'.
• ORIGIN Geduldig, Germany, 1909.

☼ ◊

Z 5–9

HEIGHT
18in (45cm)

SPREAD
18in (45cm)

Floribunda (Cluster-flowered bush)	

ROSA 'Margaret Merril'

Habit Vigorous, upright. **Flowers** Double, urn-shaped, 4in (10cm) across, singly and in clusters. White or palest blush-pink, opening to reveal golden stamens. **Scent** Sweet and strong. **Leaves** Leathery. Dark green. **Blooming period** Summer to autumn.
• TIPS Excellent for cutting; good for containers, beds, borders and hedging. Weather resistant.
• PARENTAGE ('Rudolph Timm' x 'Dedication') x 'Pascali'.
• ORIGIN Harkness, England, 1977.
• OTHER NAMES 'Harkuly'.

☼ ◊

Z 5–9

HEIGHT
3ft (1m)

SPREAD
2ft (60cm)

Hybrid Tea (Large-flowered bush)	

ROSA 'Pascali'

Habit Upright, rather open. **Flowers** Fully double, urn-shaped, 3½in (9cm) across. Almost pure white, but faintly flushed creamy-blush. **Scent** Very light, but fresh and sweet. **Leaves** Rather sparse, semi-glossy. Dark green. **Blooming period** Repeating throughout summer and autumn.
- TIPS Excellent for cutting; suitable for beds and borders.
- PARENTAGE 'Queen Elizabeth' x 'White Butterfly'.
- ORIGIN Lens, Belgium, 1963.
- OTHER NAMES 'Blanche Pasca', 'Lenip'.

Hybrid Tea (Large-flowered bush)	

ROSA 'Silver Wedding'

Habit Bushy, upright, but not very robust. **Flowers** Double, rounded, to 4in (10cm) across. White to creamy-white. **Scent** Light and fresh. **Leaves** Glossy. Mid-green. **Blooming period** Summer to autumn.
- TIPS Needs a fertile, well-mulched, reliably moisture-retentive soil, and a warm, sunny site to give its best.
- PARENTAGE Not recorded.
- ORIGIN Gregory, England, 1976.

☀ ◐

Z 5–9

HEIGHT
2½ft (75cm)

SPREAD
2ft (60cm)

☀ ◐

Z 5–9

HEIGHT
20in (50cm)

SPREAD
20in (50cm)

Floribunda (Cluster-flowered bush)	

ROSA 'Iceberg'

Habit Rounded, shapely, well-branched. **Flowers** Fully double, rounded, 3in (7cm) across, profusely, in clusters. Pure white, pink-flushed in hot weather. **Scent** Sweet but elusive. **Leaves** Ample, glossy. Bright green. **Blooming period** Summer to autumn.
- TIPS Excellent for cutting, exhibition, bedding, hedging, and as a standard. Best with light pruning. Leaves very subject to rabbit damage.
- PARENTAGE 'Robin Hood' x 'Virgo'.
- ORIGIN Kordes, Germany, 1958.
- OTHER NAMES 'Fée des Neiges', 'Schneewittchen'.

Floribunda (Cluster-flowered bush)	

ROSA 'Greenall's Glory'

Habit Compact, bushy. **Flowers** Semi-double, cupped, opening wide to 4in (12cm) across, borne freely in open clusters. White and blush-pink, paler on the back of the petals. **Scent** Light. **Leaves** Glossy. Mid-green. **Blooming period** From summer to autumn.
- TIPS Good for low hedges, borders and bedding. Suitable for containers.
- PARENTAGE A sport of 'Regensberg'.
- ORIGIN Kirkham, England, 1989.
- OTHER NAMES 'Kirmac'.

☀ ◐

Z 5–9

HEIGHT
2½–5ft
(75cm–
1.5m)
depending
on pruning

SPREAD
26in (65cm)
or more

☀ ◐

Z 5–9

HEIGHT
16in (40cm)

SPREAD
20in (50cm)

Hybrid Tea (Large-flowered bush)	

ROSA 'Elizabeth Harkness'

Habit Neat, bushy, upright. *Flowers* Pointed, fully double, 5in (12cm) across, perfect in bud, shapely when open. Pale ivory to blush-pink at the center, faintly amber-tinted. *Scent* Sweet and enduring. *Leaves* Abundant. Dark green. *Blooming period* Recurrently from summer to autumn.

• TIPS Perfect for cutting. Good for borders, massed plantings and for exhibition. Valued for its very shapely, perfectly-formed flowers and soft, subtle coloring. The blooms are sometimes affected by damp weather. It is a hardy and healthy rose, tolerant of a range of growing conditions and, if intended for cutting or exhibition, may be grown under glass in a cool greenhouse.

• PARENTAGE 'Red Dandy' x 'Piccadilly'.
• ORIGIN Harkness, England, 1969.

☼ ◊

Z 5–9

HEIGHT
2½ft (75cm)

SPREAD
2ft (60cm)

Floribunda
(Cluster-flowered bush)

ROSA 'Valentine Heart'

Habit Neat, compact, bushy. **Flowers** Semi-double, cupped to rounded, 3in (8cm) across, borne in many-flowered clusters. Blush-pink, opening from pale scarlet buds. **Scent** Sweetly fragrant. **Leaves** Plentiful, glossy. Dark green. **Blooming period** Throughout summer and autumn.
- TIPS Good for bedding, borders, massed plantings, and low hedging.
- PARENTAGE 'Shona' x 'Pot o' Gold'.
- ORIGIN Dickson, Northern Ireland, 1990.
- OTHER NAMES 'Dicogle'.

☀ ◊

Z 5–9

HEIGHT
24in (60cm)

SPREAD
20in (50cm)

Floribunda
(Cluster-flowered bush)

ROSA 'City of London'

Habit Rounded, irregular. **Flowers** Urn-shaped, loosely double, 3in (8cm) across, in dainty, open clusters. Blush-pink.**Scent** Sweet, long-lasting. **Leaves** Plentiful, glossy. Clear green. **Blooming period** Summer to autumn.
- TIPS Excellent for showing, cutting, borders, and beds. If pruned lightly, it forms a shrub, or can be trained as a climber. Goes well with old garden roses.
- PARENTAGE 'New Dawn' x 'Radox Bouquet'.
- ORIGIN Harkness, England, 1988.
- OTHER NAMES 'Harukfore'.

☀ ◊

Z 5–9

HEIGHT
3–6ft
(1–2m)

SPREAD
2½–4ft
(75cm–
1.2m)

Hybrid Tea
(Large-flowered bush)

ROSA 'Royal Highness'

Habit Upright. **Flowers** Fully double, high-centered, rounded, 5in (12cm) across, on sturdy stems. Light pearl-pink. **Scent** Strong and sweet. **Leaves** Leathery, glossy. Dark green. **Blooming period** From summer to autumn.
- TIPS Tends to "ball" in wet weather. Good for exhibition, cutting, and for mixed borders.
- PARENTAGE 'Virgo' x 'Peace'.
- ORIGIN Swim and Weeks, US, 1962.
- OTHER NAMES 'Koenigliche Hoheit'.

☀ ◊

Z 5–9

HEIGHT
3½ft (1.1m)

SPREAD
2ft (60cm)

Floribunda
(Cluster-flowered bush)

ROSA 'Queen Elizabeth'

Habit Vigorous, upright, tall. **Flowers** Fully double, rounded, opening cupped, 4in (10cm) across, singly, or in large clusters. Cyclamen-pink, **Scent** Light. **Leaves** Large, leathery, glossy. Dark green. **Blooming period** Summer to autumn.
- TIPS Excellent for cutting and for the back of a mixed border. Prune hard annually to restrict size, and maintain a dense habit. Robust and reliable.
- PARENTAGE 'Charlotte Armstrong' x 'Floradora'.
- ORIGIN Lammerts, US, 1954.
- OTHER NAMES 'The Queen Elizabeth Rose'.

☀ ◊

Z 5–9

HEIGHT
5ft (1.5m)

SPREAD
2½ft (75cm)

Floribunda (Cluster-flowered bush)	

ROSA 'Iced Ginger'

Habit Upright, open, branching. **Flowers** Fully double, pointed, 4½in (11cm) across, borne singly, and in clusters. Soft coppery-pink, with buff and ivory tints. **Scent** Very light. **Leaves** Sparse, red-tinted, mid-green. **Blooming period** From summer to autumn.
• TIPS Grows best if carefully pruned to shape and kept weed-free and well mulched. Good for placing at the back of a border and for cutting.
• PARENTAGE Seedling of 'Anne Watkins'.
• ORIGIN Dickson, Northern Ireland, 1971.

☀ ◊

Z 5–9

HEIGHT 3ft (1m)

SPREAD 28in (70cm)

Hybrid Tea (Large-flowered bush)	

ROSA 'Savoy Hotel'

Habit Vigorous, bushy, free-flowering. **Flowers** Fully double, urn-shaped, opening rounded; 4–6in (10–15cm) across. Light pink, darker on the reverse. **Scent** Fresh. **Leaves** Plentiful, semi-glossy. Dark green. **Blooming period** Summer to autumn.
• TIPS Excellent for cutting, and good for exhibition. Suitable for beds and borders and as a standard. Best in an open, sunny site and fertile soil.
• PARENTAGE 'Silver Jubilee' x 'Amber Queen'.
• ORIGIN Harkness, England, 1989.
• OTHER NAMES 'Harvintage', 'Integrity'.

☀ ◊

Z 5–9

HEIGHT 3ft (1m)

SPREAD 2ft (60cm)

Floribunda (Cluster-flowered bush)	

ROSA 'English Miss'

Habit Upright, bushy. **Flowers** Fully double, cupped, camellia-like, 3in (8cm) across, in large, dense clusters, perfect in bud and when fully open. Soft blush-pink. **Scent** Strong and spicy. **Leaves** Dense, leathery, lustrous. Dark green, purple-tinted. **Blooming period** Recurrently from summer to autumn.
• TIPS Weather resistant and easy to grow. Good for borders, low hedging, and for containers.
• PARENTAGE 'Dearest' x 'Sweet Repose'.
• ORIGIN Cant, England, 1978.

☀ ◊

Z 5–9

HEIGHT 2½ft (75cm)

SPREAD 2ft (60cm)

Floribunda (Cluster-flowered bush)	

ROSA 'Nathalie Nypels'

Habit Bushy, dense, spreading. **Flowers** Semi-double, cupped, 2in (5cm) or more across, borne in clusters. Rose-pink. **Scent** Sweet and moderately strong. **Leaves** Ample, small, glossy. Dark green. **Blooming period** From summer to autumn.
• TIPS Excellent for borders. Deadhead regularly, and prune lightly.
• PARENTAGE 'Orléans Rose' x ('Comtesse du Cayla' x R. foetida 'Bicolor').
• ORIGIN Leenders, The Netherlands, 1919.
• OTHER NAMES 'Mevrouw Nathalie Nypels'.

☀ ◊

Z 5–9

HEIGHT 2½ft (75cm)

SPREAD 2ft (60cm)

Hybrid Tea	
(Large-flowered bush)	

ROSA 'Paul Shirville'

Habit Spreading, fairly dense. *Flowers* Fully double, pointed, 3½in (9cm) across. Rosy salmon-pink. *Scent* Sweet and very pleasing. *Leaves* Plentiful, glossy. Dark green, red-tinted. *Blooming period* From summer to autumn.
• TIPS Good for cutting, bedding, mixed borders, and as a standard. Best on fertile, well-mulched soils, in a warm, sunny site.
• PARENTAGE 'Compassion' x 'Mischief'.
• ORIGIN Harkness, England, 1983.
• OTHER NAMES 'Harqueterwife', 'Heart Throb'.

☼ ◊

Z 5–9

HEIGHT
2½ft (75cm)

SPREAD
2½ft (75cm)

Hybrid Tea	
(Large-flowered bush)	

ROSA 'Julia's Rose'

Habit Open, upright, not robust. *Flowers* Double, urn-shaped, 4in (10cm) across, with slightly frilled petals opening to reveal a boss of dark stamens. Coppery-bronze on a parchment ground, with brownish-pink tints. *Scent* Light, fresh, minimal when fully open. *Leaves* Glossy. Dark green, red-tinted. *Blooming period* Summer to autumn.
• TIPS Needs fertile, well-drained soil and full sun. Attractive at all stages; perfect for cutting.
• PARENTAGE 'Blue Moon' x 'Dr. A.J. Verhage'.
• ORIGIN Wisbech Plant Co., England, 1976.

☼ ◊

Z 5–9

HEIGHT
30in (75cm)

SPREAD
18in (45cm)

Floribunda	
(Cluster-flowered bush)	

ROSA 'Elizabeth of Glamis'

Habit Upright, not vigorous. *Flowers* Cupped, double, 4–6in (10–15cm) across, with slightly frilled and scalloped petals, borne in well-spaced clusters. Soft salmon-orange. *Scent* Good, sweet. *Leaves* Semi-glossy. Mid-green. *Blooming period* Throughout summer and autumn.
• TIPS Needs fertile, well-cultivated soil, and a sheltered site. Good for borders.
• PARENTAGE 'Spartan' x 'Highlight'.
• ORIGIN McGredy, Northern Ireland, 1964.
• OTHER NAMES 'Irish Beauty'.

☼ ◊

Z 5–9

HEIGHT
2½ft (75cm)

SPREAD
2ft (60cm)

Floribunda (Cluster-flowered bush)	

ROSA 'In the Pink'

Habit Bushy, neat. *Flowers* Double, pointed buds opening high-centered, 3½ in (9cm) across. Pink and cream, deepening to coral-pink. *Scent* Sweet. *Leaves* Plentiful. Mid-green. *Blooming period* Repeatedly from summer to autumn.
• TIPS Good for cutting, bedding, borders, and hedges.
• PARENTAGE 'Carol Ann' x seedling.
• ORIGIN Pearce, England, 1994.
• OTHER NAMES 'Peaverity'.

☼ ◊

Z 5–9

HEIGHT
2ft (60cm)

SPREAD
2ft (60m)

Hybrid Tea (Large-flowered bush)	

ROSA 'Lovely Lady'

Habit Upright, bushy. *Flowers* Fully double, pointed, 4in (10cm) across, weighing down branches. Rosy-pink. *Scent* Sweet. *Leaves* Plentiful, glossy. Mid-green. *Blooming period* Summer to autumn.
• TIPS Excellent for bedding, borders, and hedges; good for cutting and exhibition. Best on fertile soil, in full sun, with moderately hard pruning.
• PARENTAGE 'Silver Jubilee' x ('Eurorose' x 'Korbell').
• ORIGIN Dickson, Northern Ireland, 1986.
• OTHER NAMES 'Dickson's Jubilee', 'Dicjubell'.

☼ ◊

Z 5–9

HEIGHT
32in (80cm)

SPREAD
28in (70cm)

Hybrid Tea (Large-flowered bush)	

ROSA 'Congratulations'

Habit Upright, vigorous. *Flowers* Urn-shaped, fully double, 4½in (11cm) across, long-stemmed. Deep rose-pink. *Scent* Light and sweet. *Leaves* Large, glossy. Dark green. *Blooming period* From summer to autumn.
• TIPS Good for cutting, exhibition, and bedding. Shows good disease resistance, and will tolerate poorer soils.
• PARENTAGE 'Carina' x seedling.
• ORIGIN Kordes, Germany, 1978.
• OTHER NAMES 'Korlift', 'Sylvia'.

☼ ◊

Z 5–9

HEIGHT
4–6ft
(1.2–2m)

SPREAD
3ft (1m)

Floribunda (Cluster-flowered bush)	

ROSA 'Hannah Gordon'

Habit Open, bushy. *Flowers* Semi-double, cupped, 3in (8cm) across, borne in clusters. Creamy-white, shading to cherry-pink at the petal edge, the color is deeper in warm weather. *Scent* Light and sweet. *Leaves* Plentiful, large, glossy. Dark green. *Blooming period* Throughout summer and autumn.
• TIPS Good for cutting, containers, bedding, and borders. Healthy, weather resistant.
• PARENTAGE Seedling x 'Bordure'.
• ORIGIN Kordes, Germany, 1983.
• OTHER NAMES 'Korweiso', 'Raspberry Ice'.

☼ ◊

Z 5–9

HEIGHT
32in (80cm)

SPREAD
26in (65cm)

Floribunda (Cluster-flowered bush)	

ROSA 'Sexy Rexy'

Habit Dense, upright. *Flowers* Fully double, cupped, opening rather flat and camellia-like, 3in (8cm) across, borne in abundant clusters just above the foliage. Light rose-pink. *Scent* Light and fresh. *Leaves* Plentiful, glossy. Dark green. *Blooming period* Throughout summer and autumn.

• TIPS Good for cutting, beds, borders, massed plantings, in containers, and as a standard. Excellent for exhibitions. This is an extremely versatile rose with beautifully formed flowers that are liable to bow down after rain. Deadhead regularly throughout the flowering season and prune in winter. Remove any dead or diseased wood, and reduce remaining stems by up to half their length.

• PARENTAGE 'Seaspray' × 'Dreaming'.
• ORIGIN McGredy, New Zealand, 1984.
• OTHER NAMES 'Macrexy', 'Heckenzauber'.

☼ ◊

Z 5–9

HEIGHT
2ft (60cm)

SPREAD
2ft (60cm)

Hybrid Tea (Large-flowered bush)	

ROSA 'Pink Favorite'

Habit Vigorous, bushy, well-branched. *Flowers* Double, opening loosely cupped from long buds, 4in (10cm) across, freely produced. Bright rose-pink. *Scent* Light and sweet. *Leaves* Narrow, glossy. Pale green. *Blooming period* Summer to autumn.
• TIPS Normally disease resistant. Best in a sunny, sheltered site. Good for exhibition, borders, and beds.
• PARENTAGE 'Juno' x ('Georg Arends' x 'New Dawn').
• ORIGIN Von Abrams, US, 1956.
• OTHER NAMES 'Pink Favourite'.

☼ ◊

Z 5–9

HEIGHT
2½ft (75cm)

SPREAD
2ft (60cm)

Floribunda (Cluster-flowered bush)	

ROSA 'Anna Livia'

Habit Dense, bushy. *Flowers* Neat, rounded, double, 2–4in (5–10cm) across, in large clusters. Clear pink. *Scent* Light and sweet. *Leaves* Abundant, leathery. Dark green. *Blooming period* From summer to autumn.
• TIPS Tolerant of a range of soils and conditions. Good for exhibition, bedding, and low hedging.
• PARENTAGE Unknown.
• ORIGIN Kordes, Germany, 1985.
• OTHER NAMES 'Kormetter', 'Trier 2000'.

☼ ◊

Z 5–9

HEIGHT
2½ft (75cm)

SPREAD
2ft (60cm)

Hybrid Tea (Large-flowered bush)	

ROSA 'Prima Ballerina'

Habit Vigorous, upright. *Flowers* Double, pointed in bud, opening rounded to 4in (10cm) across. Rose-pink, yellow-tinted, fading with age. *Scent* Strong, sweet. *Leaves* Glossy. Dark green, tinted bronze. *Blooming period* Summer to autumn.
• TIPS Suitable for beds, borders, and hedging. Weather resistant, but may be susceptible to mildew. Best in a warm, sunny site.
• PARENTAGE Seedling x 'Peace'.
• ORIGIN Tantau, Germany, 1957.
• OTHER NAMES 'Première Ballerine'.

☼ ◊

Z 5–9

HEIGHT
3ft (1m)

SPREAD
2ft (60cm)

Floribunda (Cluster-flowered bush)	

ROSA 'Dearest'

Habit Vigorous, bushy, spreading. *Flowers* Full of petals, rounded, camellia-shaped, 3in (8cm) across. Clear rose-pink. *Scent* Rich and sweet. *Leaves* Glossy. Dark-green. *Blooming period* From summer to autumn.
• TIPS Good for bedding, borders and for exhibition. Rather susceptible to blackspot.
• PARENTAGE Seedling x 'Spartan'.
• ORIGIN Dickson, Northern Ireland, 1960.

☼ ◊

Z 5–9

HEIGHT
2ft (60cm)

SPREAD
2ft (60cm)

Hybrid Tea (Large-flowered bush)

ROSA 'Blessings'

Habit Vigorous, upright, very free-flowering. **Flowers** Fully double, urn-shaped, 4in (10cm) across, borne singly, and in clusters. Soft coral-pink. **Scent** Faint but sweet. **Leaves** Large. Mid-green, on dark stems. **Blooming period** Recurrently throughout summer and autumn.

• TIPS Robust and disease resistant. Good for cutting and for borders or massed plantings.
• PARENTAGE 'Queen Elizabeth' x seedling.
• ORIGIN Gregory, England, 1968.

☼: ◊

Z 5–9

HEIGHT
3ft (1m)

SPREAD
2½ft (75cm)

Hybrid Tea (Large-flowered bush)

ROSA 'Silver Jubilee'

Habit Dense, upright, free-flowering. **Flowers** Fully double, pointed, 4–5in (10–12cm) across. Soft salmon-pink, shaded coppery, peach-pink. **Scent** Light and fresh. **Leaves** Plentiful, large, glossy. Dark green. **Blooming period** From summer to autumn.

• TIPS Good for cutting, beds, and borders. An exceptionally robust rose noted for its generosity· of bloom. May be prone to blackspot.
• PARENTAGE Seedling x 'Mischief'.
• ORIGIN Cocker, Scotland, 1978.

☼: ◊

Z 5–9

HEIGHT
3½ft (1.1m)

SPREAD
2½ft (75cm)

Floribunda (Cluster-flowered bush)

ROSA 'Anisley Dickson'

Habit Vigorous, bushy. **Flowers** Pointed, double, 3in (8cm) across, in large clusters. Salmon-pink. **Scent** Sweet but faint. **Leaves** Glossy. Dark green. **Blooming period** Repeats reliably throughout summer and early autumn.

• TIPS Suitable for exhibition, containers, bedding, and borders.
• PARENTAGE 'Coventry Cathedral' x 'Memento'.
• ORIGIN Dickson, Northern Ireland, 1983
• OTHER NAMES 'Dickimono', 'Dicky', 'Münchner Kindl'.

☼: ◊

Z 5–9

HEIGHT
3ft (1m)

SPREAD
2½ft (75cm)

Hybrid Tea (Large-flowered bush)

ROSA 'Keepsake'

Habit Bushy, upright, rather uneven. **Flowers** Fully double, rounded, 5in (12cm) across, with reflexed petals when fully open. Shades of rose-pink. **Scent** Moderate, fresh, sweet. **Leaves** Plentiful, glossy. Dark green. **Blooming period** From summer to autumn.

• TIPS Weather resistant. Useful for bedding borders, and hedges; good for exhibition.
• PARENTAGE Seedling x 'Red Planet'.
• ORIGIN Kordes, Germany. 1980.
• OTHER NAMES 'Esmeralda', 'Kormalda'.

☼: ◊

Z 5–9

HEIGHT
2½ft (75cm)

SPREAD
2ft (60cm)

Floribunda (Cluster-flowered bush)	

ROSA 'Escapade'

Habit Dense, shrubby. *Flowers* Semi-double, cupped, 3in (8cm) across, borne in large, well-spaced sprays. Rose-violet, with a white center. *Scent* Light, fresh and sweet. *Leaves* Plentiful, glossy. Mid-green. *Blooming period* Summer to autumn.

• TIPS Sturdy, reliable, disease- and weather resistant. Suitable for cutting; good for exhibition, and excellent for mixed borders. A dainty-flowered rose with a natural appearance and long flowering period, it is invaluable for enhancing the season of interest in a mixed border, where it associates well with perennials that have creamy-white, rose-pink, or deep blue flowers. It also integrates well into less formal plantings.

• PARENTAGE 'Pink Parfait' x 'Baby Faurax'.
• ORIGIN Harkness, England, 1967.
• OTHER NAMES 'Harpade'.

☼ ◊

Z 5–9

HEIGHT
32–48in
(80cm–
1.2m)

SPREAD
28in (65cm)

Hybrid Tea (Large-flowered bush)	

ROSA 'Abbeyfield Rose'

Habit Compact, bushy. *Flowers* Fully double, pointed, to 4in (10cm) across, with rather few petals, but elegantly set around a high-pointed center. Deep rose-pink. *Scent* Sweet but light. *Leaves* Abundant, glossy. Dark green. *Blooming period* Recurrently throughout summer and autumn.
• TIPS Excellent for bedding, borders, and massed plantings.
• PARENTAGE 'National Trust' x 'Silver Jubilee'.
• ORIGIN Cocker, Scotland, 1985.
• OTHER NAMES 'Cocbrose'.

☼ ◊

Z 5–9

HEIGHT
2–2½ft
(60–75cm)

SPREAD
2ft (60cm)

Floribunda (Cluster-flowered bush)	

ROSA 'City of Leeds'

Habit Neat, compact, bushy. *Flowers* Cupped, double, 2–4in (5–10cm) across, in many-flowered, well-spaced clusters. Salmon-pink. *Scent* Very light. *Leaves* Large, glossy. Dark green. *Blooming period* Recurrently from summer to autumn.
• TIPS Best if hard-pruned in the first year and moderately thereafter. Good for exhibition and bedding.
• PARENTAGE 'Evelyn Fison' x ('Spartan' x 'Red Favourite').
• ORIGIN McGredy, Northern Ireland, 1966.

☼ ◊

Z 5–9

HEIGHT
2½ft (75cm)

SPREAD
2ft (60cm)

Floribunda (Cluster-flowered bush)	

ROSA 'Regensberg'

Habit Neat, compact, bushy. *Flowers* Double, cupped, 5in (12cm) across, borne in large, open clusters. Light pink, with a white eye and petal edge, and a paler pink petal reverse. *Scent* Light. *Leaves* Glossy. Light green. *Blooming period* Summer to autumn.
• TIPS Excellent for bedding and massed plantings.
• PARENTAGE 'Geoff Boycott' x 'Old Master'.
• ORIGIN McGredy, New Zealand, 1979.
• OTHER NAMES 'Macyoumis', 'Buffalo Bill', 'Young Mistress'.

☼ ◊

Z 5–9

HEIGHT
16in (40cm)

SPREAD
20in (50cm)

Floribunda (Cluster-flowered bush)	

ROSA 'Piccolo'

Habit Bushy, compact. *Flowers* Double, rounded, 2½in (6cm) across, opening from neat, rounded buds, and freely borne in many-flowered clusters. Bright tomato-red. *Scent* Little. *Leaves* Glossy. Mid-green, tinted with red. *Blooming period* From summer to autumn.
• TIPS Good for beds, front of borders, and low hedging. Weather resistant.
• PARENTAGE Not disclosed.
• ORIGIN Tantau, Germany, 1984.
• OTHER NAMES 'Piccola', 'Tanolokip'.

☼ ◊

Z 5–9

HEIGHT
20in (50cm)

SPREAD
20in (50cm)

Floribunda (Cluster-flowered bush)	

ROSA 'Fred Loads'

Habit Vigorous, upright, tall. **Flowers** Semi-double, cupped, 2–4in (5–10cm) across, borne in large clusters. Strong vermilion-orange. **Scent** Moderate. **Leaves** Plentiful, large. Mid-green. **Blooming period** Repeats from summer to autumn.
• TIPS Robust and disease resistant; excellent for exhibition, and useful for larger gardens and screens. Produces plentiful new shoots from the base.
• PARENTAGE Probably 'Dorothy Wheatcroft' × 'Orange Sensation'.
• ORIGIN Holmes, England, 1967.

☼ ◌

Z 5–9

HEIGHT
6ft (2m)

SPREAD
3ft (1m)

Hybrid Tea (Large-flowered bush)	

ROSA 'Super Star' Tropicana

Habit Vigorous, uneven, well-branched, free-flowering. **Flowers** Double, pointed, 5in (12cm) across. Vermilion to pale scarlet. **Scent** Light and fresh. **Leaves** Semi-glossy. Mid-green. **Blooming period** Summer to autumn.
• TIPS Suitable for bedding and borders, but strong color needs careful placement. Prone to mildew.
• PARENTAGE (Seedling × 'Peace') × (seedling × 'Alpine Glow'.
• ORIGIN Tantau, Germany, 1960.
• OTHER NAMES 'Tanorstar', 'Tropicana'.

☼ ◌

Z 5–9

HEIGHT
3½ft (1.1m)

SPREAD
3ft (1m)

Hybrid Tea (Large-flowered bush)	

ROSA 'Mischief'

Habit Vigorous, upright, floriferous. **Flowers** Double, urn-shaped, 4in (10cm) across. Salmon-pink; autumn flowers are of a darker hue. **Scent** Light. **Leaves** Plentiful, light green. **Blooming period** From summer to autumn.
• TIPS Good for cutting, bedding, borders, or in containers. Generally healthy but is susceptible to rust.
• PARENTAGE 'Peace' × 'Spartan'.
• ORIGIN McGredy, Northern Ireland, 1961.
• OTHER NAMES 'Macmi'.

☼ ◌

Z 5–9

HEIGHT
3ft (1m)

SPREAD
2ft (60cm)

Hybrid Tea (Large-flowered bush)	

ROSA 'Precious Platinum'

Habit Vigorous, bushy, uneven. **Flowers** Fully double, rounded, 4in (10cm) across, on strong stems. Deep, bright crimson scarlet. **Scent** Light. **Leaves** Abundant, semi-glossy, leathery. Mid-green. **Blooming period** From summer to autumn.
• TIPS Excellent for bedding, borders, hedging, and containers, and good for cutting and exhibition. May also be grown under glass.
• PARENTAGE 'Red Planet' × 'Franklin Engelmann'.
• ORIGIN Dickson, Northern Ireland, 1974.
• OTHER NAMES 'Opa Pötschke', 'Red Star'.

☼ ◌

Z 5–9

HEIGHT
3ft (1m)

SPREAD
2ft (60cm)

Hybrid Tea (Large-flowered bush)

ROSA 'Fragrant Cloud'

Habit Dense, bushy. *Flowers* Large, double, rounded, 5in (12cm) across. Aging from coral-red, through dusky scarlet to purplish-red. *Scent* Strong and pleasing. *Leaves* Abundant, large, leathery. Dark green. *Blooming period* Recurrently from summer to autumn.
• TIPS Good for massed plantings, cutting, and exhibition. With its long and reliable flowering period and dense and strongly upright habit, it is particularly suited to beds in a formal rose garden. A generally hardy and healthy rose with a remarkably strong scent, although the flowers have a tendency to "ball" in wet weather. In hot conditions, the flowers develop strong purplish-red tones as they fade.
• PARENTAGE Seedling × 'Prima Ballerina'.
• ORIGIN Tantau, Germany, 1963.
• OTHER NAMES 'Duftwolke', 'Nuage Parfumé', 'Tanellis'.

☼ ◊

Z 5–9

HEIGHT
2½ft (75cm)

SPREAD
2ft (60cm)

Hybrid Tea (Large-flowered bush)	

ROSA 'Royal William'

Habit Vigorous, upright. **Flowers** Fully double, pointed, 5in (12cm) across, long-stemmed. Deep crimson. **Scent** Sweet. **Leaves** Large, semi-glossy. Dark green. **Blooming period** Summer to autumn.
• TIPS Perfect for cutting, although flower quality is variable through the season. Good for bedding, borders, and as a standard.
• PARENTAGE 'Feuerzauber' x seedling.
• ORIGIN Kordes, Germany, 1984.
• OTHER NAMES 'Duftzauber '84', 'Korzaun', 'Fragrant Charm '84'.

☀ ◊

Z 5–9

HEIGHT
3ft (1m)

SPREAD
2½ft (75cm)

Floribunda (Cluster-flowered bush)	

ROSA 'Disco Dancer'

Habit Bushy, dense. **Flowers** Semi-double, cupped, 2⅓in (6cm) across, in many-flowered clusters. Vivid orange-scarlet. **Scent** Very light. **Leaves** Plentiful, glossy. Dark green. **Blooming period** Throughout summer to autumn.
• TIPS Excellent for a bed of one variety; good for hedging and, if pruned to shape, may be grown in a container.
• PARENTAGE 'Coventry Cathedral' x 'Memento'.
• ORIGIN Dickson, Northern Ireland, 1984.
• OTHER NAMES 'Dicinfra'.

☀ ◊

Z 5–9

HEIGHT
2½ft (75cm)

SPREAD
2ft (60cm)

Hybrid Tea (Large-flowered bush)	

ROSA 'Double Delight'

Habit Bushy, lanky, free-branching. **Flowers** Rounded, fully double, 5in (12cm) across. Creamy-white, edged and flushed carmine-pink. **Scent** Strong, sweet. **Leaves** Abundant. Mid-green. **Blooming period** Repeats from summer to autumn.
• TIPS Does well under glass, or outdoors in warm, dry weather, as blooms are spoiled by rain. Good for exhibition and cutting.
• PARENTAGE 'Granada' x 'Garden Party'.
• ORIGIN Swim and Ellis, US, 1977.
• OTHER NAMES 'Andeli'.

☀ ◊

Z 5–9

HEIGHT
3ft (1m)

SPREAD
2ft (60cm)

Floribunda (Cluster-flowered bush)	

ROSA 'Melody Maker'

Habit Bushy, dense, upright. **Flowers** Double, rounded, 3½in (9cm) across, borne in many-flowered clusters that nestle among the foliage. Light red-vermilion. **Scent** Light. **Leaves** Plentiful, glossy, dark green. **Blooming period** From summer to autumn.
• TIPS Suitable for containers, bedding, and borders. Can be grown as a standard. May be prone to mildew.
• PARENTAGE Seedling of 'Anisley Dickson'.
• ORIGIN Dickson, Northern Ireland, 1991.
• OTHER NAMES 'Dicqueen'.

☀ ◊

Z 5–9

HEIGHT
28in (70cm)

SPREAD
2ft (60cm)

Hybrid Tea (Large-flowered bush)	

ROSA 'Loving Memory'

Habit Robust, upright. *Flowers* Fully double, pointed, 5in (12cm) across, deep, bright, red-crimson, on long, strong stems. *Scent* Light and sweet. *Leaves* Large. Deep green. *Blooming period* From summer to autumn.
• TIPS Excellent for exhibition, and good for large borders and beds.
• PARENTAGE Seedling × 'Red Planet' seedling.
• ORIGIN Kordes, Germany, 1981.
• OTHER NAMES 'Red Cedar', 'Burgund '81', 'Korgund '81'.

☼ ◊

Z 5–9

HEIGHT
3½ft (1.1m)

SPREAD
2½ft (75cm)

Floribunda (Cluster-flowered bush)	

ROSA 'Lilli Marlene'

Habit Vigorous, bushy, well-branched, and thorny. *Flowers* Double, rounded, 3in (8cm) across, borne in large clusters. Rich bright scarlet-crimson. *Scent* Very light. *Leaves* Glossy. Bronze-tinted, dark green. *Blooming period* Summer and autumn.
• TIPS Good for exhibition, hedging, bedding, and borders. Generally healthy but slightly susceptible to blackspot.
• PARENTAGE ('Our Princess' × 'Rudolph Timm') × 'Ama'.
• ORIGIN Kordes, Germany, 1959.

☼ ◊

Z 5–9

HEIGHT
28in (70cm)

SPREAD
24in (60cm)

Floribunda (Cluster-flowered bush)	

ROSA 'Matangi'

Habit Bushy, shapely, dense. *Flowers* Double, cupped, open, to 3½in (9cm) across, borne in large sprays. Bright orange-vermilion, with a silvery-white eye and a silvery petal reverse. *Scent* Light. *Leaves* Plentiful, glossy. Dark green. *Blooming period* From summer to autumn.
• TIPS Hardy and healthy, especially if well mulched. Good for exhibition, bedding, and borders.
• PARENTAGE Seedling × 'Picasso'.
• ORIGIN McGredy, New Zealand, 1974.
• OTHER NAMES 'Macman'.

☼ ◊

Z 5–9

HEIGHT
32in (80cm)

SPREAD
2ft (60cm)

Floribunda (Cluster-flowered bush)	

ROSA 'Tango'

Habit Dense, upright. **Flowers** Semi-double, cupped, 2–4in (5–10cm) across, with slightly frilled petals. Orange-scarlet, fading to white at the rim, yellow at the base, with a pale yellow petal reverse **Scent** Little. **Leaves** Plentiful, large. Dark green. **Blooming period** Summer to autumn.•
• TIPS Good for cutting, bedding, and containers.
• PARENTAGE 'Sexy Rexy' x 'Maestro'
• ORIGIN McGredy, New Zealand,1988.
• OTHER NAMES 'Macfirwal', 'Rock 'n' Roll', 'Stretch Johnson'.

☼ ◊

Z 5–9

HEIGHT
2½ft (75cm)

SPREAD
2ft (60cm)

Hybrid Tea (Large-flowered bush)	

ROSA 'National Trust'

Habit Compact, bushy, upright, free-flowering. **Flowers** Fully double, urn-shaped, 4in (10cm) across, borne singly and in clusters. Unfading scarlet-crimson. **Scent** Very little. **Leaves** Plentiful, matte. Dark green, red-tinted. **Blooming period** From summer to autumn.
• TIPS Good for bedding, borders and containers.
• PARENTAGE 'Evelyn Fison' x 'King of Hearts'.
• ORIGIN McGredy, Northern Ireland, 1970.
• OTHER NAMES 'Bad Nauheim'.

☼ ◊

Z 5–9

HEIGHT
2ft (60cm)

SPREAD
2ft (60cm)

Hybrid Tea (Large-flowered bush)	

ROSA 'Papa Meilland'

Habit Upright, lanky. **Flowers** Double, pointed, to 6in (15cm) across, high-centered and well-formed. Pure dark crimson. **Scent** Sweet, heavy. **Leaves** Large, leathery. Dark green. **Blooming period** Repeating from summer to autumn.
• TIPS Good for cutting and exhibition, but rather prone to mildew, blackspot, and winter die-back. Best in very fertile soil and a sheltered site.
• PARENTAGE 'Chrysler Imperial' x 'Charles Mallerin'.
• ORIGIN Meilland, France, 1963.
• OTHER NAMES 'Meisar'.

☼ ◊

Z 5–9

HEIGHT
3ft (1m)

SPREAD
2ft (60cm)

Floribunda (Cluster-flowered bush)	

ROSA 'The Times Rose'

Habit Spreading, compact, even growth. **Flowers** Double, cupped, 3–4in (8–10cm) across. Deep crimson, opening to reveal a boss of yellow stamens. **Scent** Light. **Leaves** Plentiful, thick, glossy. Purplish-green. **Blooming period** Summer and autumn.
• TIPS Good for cutting, exhibition, containers, bedding, hedging, and massed plantings.
• PARENTAGE 'Tornado' x 'Redgold'
• ORIGIN Kordes, Germany, 1984.
• OTHER NAMES 'Mariandel', 'Carl Philip', 'Christian IV', 'Korpeahn'.

☼ ◊

Z 5–9

HEIGHT
2ft (60cm)
or more

SPREAD
2½ft (75cm)

Dwarf cluster-flowered bush (Patio bush)

ROSA 'Drummer Boy'

Habit Bushy, spreading. *Flowers* Cupped, semi-double, 2in (5cm) across, with slightly frilled petals, borne in dense, profuse clusters. Deep bright crimson. *Scent* Faint. *Leaves* Small but abundant. Dark green. *Blooming period* Summer to autumn.

• TIPS A good choice for low hedging or in the front of a mixed border or rose bed. The profusion of richly colored, frilled flowers is also displayed to good effect if planted in tubs or large pots to decorate a patio, or other paved or graveled areas

in the garden. It is a sturdy, robust, and healthy rose, with attractive and abundant foliage, and a long and reliable flowering period that proves especially valuable for its resistance to extremes of weather.

• PARENTAGE Seedling x 'Red Sprite'.
• ORIGIN Harkness, England, 1987.
• OTHER NAMES 'Harvacity'.

☀ ◊

Z 5–9

HEIGHT
20in (50cm)

SPREAD
20in (50cm)

Hybrid Tea (Large-flowered bush)	

ROSA 'Alec's Red'

Habit Vigorous, bushy, freely branching.
Flowers Fully double, pointed, 6in (15cm) or
more across. Deep crimson to rich cherry red.
Scent Sweet, rich, and heavy. **Leaves** On thorny
stems. Dark green. **Blooming period** Recurrently
throughout summer and autumn.
• TIPS Excellent for cutting and exhibition. Good
for borders, hedging, and massed plantings.
• PARENTAGE 'Fragrant Cloud' × 'Dame de Coeur'.
• ORIGIN Cocker, Scotland, 1970.
• OTHER NAMES 'Cored'.

☼ ◊

Z 5–9

HEIGHT
3ft (1m)

SPREAD
2ft (60cm)

Floribunda (Cluster-flowered bush)	

ROSA 'Glad Tidings'

Habit Upright, compact, bushy. **Flowers**
Double, cupped, with velvety petals, borne
in neat, well-spaced clusters. Rich dark crimson.
Scent Light. **Leaves** Very glossy. Dark
green. **Blooming period** Recurrently
throughout summer.
• TIPS Susceptible to blackspot, but otherwise
robust. Suitable for borders and hedging.
• PARENTAGE Not disclosed.
• ORIGIN Tantau, Germany, 1988.
• OTHER NAMES 'Tantide'.

☼ ◊

Z 5–9

HEIGHT
2½ft (75cm)

SPREAD
2ft (60cm)

Hybrid Tea (Large-flowered bush)	

ROSA 'Red Devil'

Habit Vigorous, bushy. **Flowers** Fully double,
pointed, 6in (15cm) or more across. Rose-scarlet,
with a paler petal reverse. **Scent** Sweet. **Leaves**
Large, glossy. Dark green. **Blooming period**
Summer to autumn.
• TIPS Good for cutting and exhibition, but
blooms are quickly spoiled by rain.
• PARENTAGE 'Silver Lining' × 'Prima Ballerina'
seedling.
• ORIGIN Dickson. Northern Ireland, 1967.
• OTHER NAMES 'Coeur d'Amour'.

☼ ◊

Z 5–9

HEIGHT
3ft (1m)

SPREAD
2½ft (75cm)

Hybrid Tea (Large-flowered bush)	

ROSA 'Ruby Wedding'

Habit Upright, well-branched. **Flowers** Double,
rounded, to 4in (10cm) across. Clear dark ruby-
crimson. **Scent** Light and sweet. **Leaves** Rather
sparse, semi-glossy. Mid-green. **Blooming period**
Summer to autumn.
• TIPS Suitable for cutting, beds, and borders.
Grown largely for its name.
• PARENTAGE 'Mayflower' × seedling.
• ORIGIN Gregory, England, 1979.

☼ ◊

Z 5–9

HEIGHT
2½ft (75cm)

SPREAD
2ft (60cm)

Hybrid Tea (Large-flowered bush)

ROSA 'Ingrid Bergman'

Habit Upright, well-branched, irregular. *Flowers* Double, urn-shaped, 4½in (11cm) across, with velvety petals, on long stems. Clear and pure dark red. *Scent* Light. *Leaves* Leathery, semi-glossy. Dark green. *Blooming period* From summer to autumn.

• TIPS The long-stemmed and well-formed flowers are excellent for cutting. It is good for bedding, borders, and container plantings and may also be grown as a standard. This is a hardy rose that is easy to grow, and valued as one of the most dependable dark red garden roses available. The flowers are a remarkably clear red, without any hint of blue tones. Generally disease resistant, but may be prone to blackspot.

• PARENTAGE A seedling of 'Precious Platinum'.
• ORIGIN Poulsen, Denmark, 1984.
• OTHER NAMES 'Poulman'.

☼: ◊

Z 5–9

HEIGHT
30in (75cm)

SPREAD
24in (60cm)

Hybrid Tea (Large-flowered bush)	

ROSA 'Alexander'

Habit Vigorous, upright, tall. *Flowers* Pointed, double, to 5in (12cm) across, long-stemmed. Red-vermilion. *Scent* Light and sweet. *Leaves* Abundant, glossy. Dark green. *Blooming period* Recurrently throughout summer and autumn.
• TIPS One of the easiest roses to grow. The long-stemmed and well-formed flowers are good for cutting and arranging and last well, if cut while still in bud. The brilliant red-vermilion of its flowers is a very strong and luminous color that needs careful placement, if it is not to become dominant or

overpowering in the border, or clash with other strong colors. Strong, disease resistant. Good for beds, hedges, and fences.
• PARENTAGE 'Super Star' x ('Ann Elizabeth' x 'Allgold').
• ORIGIN Harkness, England, 1972.
• OTHER NAMES 'Alexandra'.

☼ ◊

Z 5–9

HEIGHT
5–6ft
(1.5–2m)

SPREAD
2½ft (75cm)

Floribunda
(Cluster-flowered bush)

ROSA 'Trumpeter'

Habit Neat and bushy. **Flowers** Fully double, cupped, 2½in (6cm) across, opening from neat, rounded buds and borne in large clusters. Rich red. **Scent** Little. **Leaves** Plentiful, glossy. Dark green. **Blooming period** Throughout summer and autumn.
• TIPS Good for mass plantings, bedding, low hedging, and containers. Also for exhibition and to grow in standard form.
• PARENTAGE 'Satchmo' x seedling.
• ORIGIN McGredy, New Zealand, 1977.
• OTHER NAMES 'Mactru'

Hybrid Tea
(Large-flowered bush)

ROSA 'Ena Harkness'

Habit Vigorous, open, upright, free-flowering. **Flowers** Fully double, urn-shaped, with high centers, 10–6in (15cm) across, with velvety petals. Deep scarlet-crimson. **Scent** Sweet and strong. **Leaves** Rather sparse. Mid-green. **Blooming period** Recurrently from early summer to autumn.
• TIPS Does best in fertile, moisture-retentive soil, in an open site. The flower stems are sometimes bowed.
• PARENTAGE 'Crimson Glory' x 'Southport'.
• ORIGIN Norman, England, 1946.

☼: ◊

Z 5–9

HEIGHT
24in (60cm)

SPREAD
20in (50cm)

☼: ◊

Z 5–9

HEIGHT
2½ft (75cm)

SPREAD
2ft (60cm)

Floribunda
(Cluster-flowered bush)

ROSA 'Evelyn Fison'

Habit Vigorous, bushy. **Flowers** Double, cupped, neatly formed, 2–4in (5–10cm) across, borne in many-flowered clusters. Bright, dark scarlet-red, and non-fading. **Scent** Little. **Leaves** Glossy. Dark green. **Blooming period** Throughout summer to autumn.
• TIPS Good for borders, bedding, massed plantings and showing. Often subject to premature leaf fall.
• PARENTAGE 'Moulin Rouge' x 'Korona'.
• ORIGIN McGredy, Northern Ireland, 1962.
• OTHER NAMES 'Macev', 'Irish Wonder'.

Floribunda
(Cluster-flowered bush)

ROSA 'Remembrance'

Habit Bushy, compact. **Flowers** Double, rounded, to 4in (10cm) across, in showy clusters. Deep bright scarlet. **Scent** Light and sweet. **Leaves** Glossy. Dark green. **Blooming period** From summer to autumn.
• TIPS Good for bedding, massed plantings, and containers. May also be grown as a standard.
• PARENTAGE 'Trumpeter' x 'Southampton'.
• ORIGIN Harkness, England, 1992.
• OTHER NAMES 'Harxampton'.

☼: ◊

Z 5–9

HEIGHT
28in (70cm)

SPREAD
24in (60cm)

☼: ◊

Z 5–9

HEIGHT
26in (65cm)

SPREAD
20in (50cm)

| Hybrid Tea | |
| (Large-flowered bush) | |

ROSA 'Deep Secret'

Habit Upright. **Flowers** Double, variable in form, often low-centered, 4–6in (10–15cm) across. Uniform deep crimson. **Scent** Rich and sweet. **Leaves** Semi-glossy. Dark green. **Blooming period** From summer to autumn.
• TIPS Good for cutting, for beds, and borders.
• PARENTAGE Not disclosed.
• ORIGIN Tantau, Germany, 1977.
• OTHER NAMES 'Mildred Scheel'.

☼ ◊

Z 5–9

HEIGHT
3ft (90cm)

SPREAD
2½ft (75cm)

| Hybrid Tea | |
| (Large-flowered bush) | |

ROSA 'Rose Gaujard'

Habit Upright, vigorous, branching, free-flowering. **Flowers** Fully double, urn-shaped, 4in (10cm) across. Carmine-red, with a paler, silvery-blush petal reverse. **Scent** Light and sweet. **Leaves** Plentiful, glossy. Dark green. **Blooming period** From summer to autumn.
• TIPS Useful for cutting and exhibition. Good for hedging and borders. Robust, healthy; easy to grow.
• PARENTAGE 'Peace' x 'Opera' seedling.
• ORIGIN Gaujard, France, 1957.
• OTHER NAMES 'Gaumo'.

☼ ◊

Z 5–9

HEIGHT
3½ft (1.1m)

SPREAD
2½ft (75cm)

| Hybrid Tea | |
| (Large-flowered bush) | |

ROSA 'Ernest H. Morse'

Habit Vigorous, upright, fairly even. **Flowers** Double, 4–6in (10–15cm) across, freely produced. Bright red-crimson, fading and becoming duller with age. **Scent** Strong and sweet. **Leaves** Plentiful, large, glossy. Dark green. **Blooming period** Repeating from summer to autumn.
• TIPS Healthy and reliable. Good for exhibition and bedding.
• PARENTAGE Not disclosed.
• ORIGIN Kordes, Germany, 1965.

☼ ◊

Z 5–9

HEIGHT
2½ft (75cm)

SPREAD
2ft (60cm)

| Hybrid Tea | |
| (Large-flowered bush) | |

ROSA 'Big Purple'

Habit Upright, free-branching. **Flowers** Double, large, high-centered, 4–6in (10–15cm) across. Bright beetroot-purple. **Scent** Heavy. **Leaves** Large. Dark green. **Blooming period** Summer to autumn.
• TIPS Good for bedding or borders, but the strong color needs careful placement. Suitable for cutting and exhibition. Sturdy, disease resistant.
• PARENTAGE Seedling x 'Purple Splendour'.
• ORIGIN Stephens, New Zealand, 1987.
• OTHER NAMES 'Stebigpu', 'Nuit d'Orient', 'Stephens' Big Purple'.

☼ ◊

Z 5–9

HEIGHT
3ft (1m)

SPREAD
2ft (60cm)

Floribunda
(Cluster-flowered bush)

ROSA 'News'

Habit Upright, fairly compact. **Flowers** Double, cupped, opening flat, 3in (8cm) across, in large clusters. Rich red-purple. **Scent** Light. **Leaves** Dense, semi-glossy. Mid-green. **Blooming period** From summer to autumn.
• TIPS Good for cutting, beds, and hedges, and suitable for containers. Weather resistant.
• PARENTAGE 'Lilac Charm' x 'Tuscany Superb'.
• ORIGIN LeGrice, England, 1968.
• OTHER NAMES 'Legnews'.

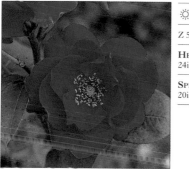

☼: ◊

Z 5–9

HEIGHT
24in (60cm)

SPREAD
20in (50cm)

Hybrid Tea
(Large-flowered bush)

ROSA 'Blue Moon'

Habit Upright, open, well-branched. **Flowers** Pointed, fully double, 4in (10cm) across, lilac-mauve, tinted blue in warm sun. **Scent** Sweet, well-scented. **Leaves** Large, glossy, mid-green. **Blooming period** Through summer and autumn.
• TIPS Best under glass or in a moist, open site. Good for exhibition, cutting, and borders.
• PARENTAGE 'Sterling Silver' seedling x seedling.
• ORIGIN Tantau, Germany, 1964.
• OTHER NAMES 'Blue Monday', 'Sissi', 'Mainzer Fastnacht', 'Tannacht'.

☼: ◊

Z 5–9

HEIGHT
3ft (1m)

SPREAD
2ft (60cm)

Floribunda
(Cluster-flowered bush)

ROSA 'Princess Alice'

Habit Upright. **Flowers** Double, rounded, 2½in (6cm) across, borne in large, strong-stemmed clusters. Bright yellow. **Scent** Light. **Leaves** Abundant, semi-glossy. Light green. **Blooming period** Summer to autumn.
• TIPS Disease and weather resistant. Good for cutting, exhibition, bedding, borders, and hedging.
• PARENTAGE 'Judy Garland' x 'Anne Harkness'.
• ORIGIN Harkness, England, 1985.
• OTHER NAMES 'Hartanna', 'Brite Lights', 'Zonta Rose'.

☼: ◊

Z 5–9

HEIGHT
3½ft (1.1m)

SPREAD
2ft (60cm)

Hybrid Tea (Large-flowered bush)	

ROSA 'Elina'

Habit Shrubby, vigorous, upright. **Flowers** Rounded, fully double, 6in (15cm) across. Ivory-white, flushed lemon at the center. **Scent** Light. **Leaves** Plentiful, large. Dark green, red-tinted. **Blooming period** Throughout summer and autumn.

• TIPS A good choice for planting in beds and borders, as well as for cutting, and exhibition. Versatile and one of the easiest roses to grow, 'Elina' is much valued for its form, clear, elegant color and long flowering period.

It was previously known as 'Peaudouce', which means "soft skin" in French, the petals have a beautiful, silky texture.

• PARENTAGE 'Nana Mouskouri' x 'Lolita'.
• ORIGIN Dickson. Northern Ireland, 1985.
• OTHER NAMES 'Dicjana', 'Peaudouce'.

☼ ◊

Z 5–9

HEIGHT
3½ft (1.1m)

SPREAD
2½ft (75cm)

Floribunda (Cluster-flowered bush)	

ROSA 'Arthur Bell'

Habit Vigorous, upright. **Flowers** Cupped, semi-double, 3in (8cm) across, with long petals, borne singly, and in clusters. Yellow, fading to pale yellow. **Scent** Strong, fruity and sweet. **Leaves** Abundant, glossy. Bright green. **Blooming period** From summer to autumn.
• TIPS For exhibition, bedding, hedging, and containers. Weather resistant, and tolerant of a range of soils and conditions. Good for cutting.
• PARENTAGE 'Cläre Grammerstorf' x 'Piccadilly'.
• ORIGIN McGredy, Northern Ireland, 1965.

☼ ◌

Z 5–9

HEIGHT
2½–3ft
(75cm–1m)

SPREAD
2ft (60cm)

Floribunda (Cluster-flowered bush)	

ROSA 'Princess Michael of Kent'

Habit Neat, bushy, compact. **Flowers** Fully double, rounded, 3½in (9cm) across, borne singly, and in clusters. Yellow. **Scent** Sweet. **Leaves** Glossy. Bright to mid-green. **Blooming period** From summer well into autumn.
• TIPS Healthy and disease resistant. Good for cutting and for beds, borders, low hedging, and containers.
• PARENTAGE 'Manx Queen' x 'Alexander'.
• ORIGIN Harkness, England, 1981.
• OTHER NAMES 'Harlightly'.

☼ ◌

Z 5–9

HEIGHT
24in (60cm)

SPREAD
20in (50cm)

Hybrid Tea (Large-flowered bush)	

ROSA 'Sunblest'

Habit Upright, bushy, compact, free-flowering. **Flowers** Double, pointed buds, opening cupped, rounded, 4in (10cm) across. Clear, unfading yellow. **Scent** Light and fresh. **Leaves** Glossy. Mid-green. **Blooming period** From summer to autumn.
• TIPS Suitable for bedding and borders.
• PARENTAGE Seedling x 'King's Ransom'.
• ORIGIN Tantau, Germany, 1970.
• OTHER NAMES 'Landora'.

☼ ◌

Z 5–9

HEIGHT
3ft (90cm)

SPREAD
2ft (60cm)

Hybrid Tea (Large-flowered bush)	

ROSA 'Dutch Gold'

Habit Vigorous, upright. **Flowers** Rounded, fully double, 6in (15cm) across. Rich golden-yellow and not fading. **Scent** Strong, sweet. **Leaves** Large. Dark green. **Blooming period** From summer to autumn.
• TIPS Healthy, disease-resistant foliage. Good for borders and for cutting and exhibition.
• PARENTAGE 'Peer Gynt' x 'Whisky Mac'.
• ORIGIN Wisbech Plant Co. England, 1978.

☼ ◌

Z 5–9

HEIGHT
3½ft (1.1m)

SPREAD
2½ft (75cm)

Hybrid Tea (Large-flowered bush)

ROSA 'Grandpa Dickson'

Habit Upright, open. *Flowers* Large, double, high-centered 7in (18cm) across. Clear pale yellow, but flushing pink in warm weather. *Scent* Light. *Leaves* Sparse, glossy. Pale green. *Blooming period* Repeating freely from summer to autumn.

• TIPS The well-formed flowers with pointed petals are good for exhibition, beds and formal borders. It repeats freely, although its foliage can appear rather sparse for a plant with such large blooms. It will do best in a site in full sun with fertile and moisture-retentive soil. Keep weed-free, and water well during prolonged periods of dry weather.

• PARENTAGE ('Perfecta' x 'Governador Braga da Cruz') x 'Piccadilly'.

• ORIGIN Dickson, Northern Ireland, 1966.

• OTHER NAMES 'Irish Gold'.

☼ ◊

Z 5–9

HEIGHT
32in (80cm)

SPREAD
24in (60cm)

Dwarf cluster-flowered bush / Patio bush

ROSA 'Baby Love'

Habit Compact, bushy, upright. *Flowers* Single, cupped, about 2in (5cm) across. Bright yellow, with prominent stamens, in open clusters. *Scent* Sweet, moderately strong. *Leaves* Abundant, small, glossy. Mid-green. *Blooming period* Summer to autumn.
• TIPS Disease resistant; free-flowering. Good for bedding, containers, and low hedging.
• PARENTAGE 'Sweet Magic' × (seedling × *Rosa davidii* var. *elongata*).
• ORIGIN Scrivens, England, 1995
• OTHER NAMES 'Scrivluv'.

☼ ◊

Z 5–9

HEIGHT
32in (80cm)

SPREAD
2ft (60cm)

Floribunda (Cluster-flowered bush)

ROSA 'Benita'

Habit Vigorous, bushy, irregular. *Flowers* Double, rounded, to 3½in (9cm) across, with frilled petal margins, in large trusses of up to 12 blooms. Deep amber-gold. *Scent* Light. *Leaves* Plentiful, medium-sized, semi-glossy. Mid-green. *Blooming period* From summer to autumn.
• TIPS Very healthy and free-blooming. Good for bedding and borders.
• PARENTAGE ('Korresia' × 'Bright Smile') × seedling.
• ORIGIN Dickson, Northern Ireland, 1995.
• OTHER NAMES 'Dicquarrel'.

☼ ◊

Z 5–9

HEIGHT
3ft (1m)

SPREAD
2ft (60cm)

Floribunda (Cluster-flowered bush)

ROSA 'Golden Wedding'

Habit Bushy. *Flowers* Double, rounded, high-centered, 5in (12cm) across, borne in clusters. Deep bright yellow with orange stamens. *Scent* Light. *Leaves* Plentiful. Glossy green. *Blooming period* From summer to autumn.
• TIPS Good for cutting, bedding and borders, and to grow in containers.
• PARENTAGE Not disclosed.
• ORIGIN Christensen, US, 1990.
• OTHER NAMES 'Arokris'.

☼ ◊

Z 5–9

HEIGHT
32in (80cm)

SPREAD
2ft (60cm)

Floribunda (Cluster-flowered bush)

ROSA 'Toprose'

Habit Upright, open. *Flowers* Double, rounded, 4in (10cm) across, borne singly, and in clusters. Bright yellow. *Scent* Light and sweet. *Leaves* Glossy. Mid-green. *Blooming period* Summer to autumn.
• TIPS Healthy, reliable, and disease resistant. Good for borders, bedding, and containers.
• PARENTAGE [('Chinatown' × 'Golden Masterpiece') × 'Adolf Horstmann'] × 'Yellow Pages'.
• ORIGIN Cocker, Scotland, 1988.
• OTHER NAMES 'Cocgold', 'Dania'.

☼ ◊

Z 5–9

HEIGHT
28in (70cm)

SPREAD
2ft (60cm)

Floribunda (Cluster-flowered bush)	

ROSA 'Korresia'

Habit Neat, compact, upright. **Flowers** Double, urn-shaped, 3in (8cm) across, with slightly waved petals, borne in neat, open clusters. Unfading, clear, bright golden-yellow. **Scent** Sweet and strong. **Leaves** Glossy. Light green. **Blooming period** From summer to autumn.
• TIPS Needs to be well-mulched and pruned fairly hard. Good for cutting, beds, and borders.
• PARENTAGE 'Friedrich Wörlein' x 'Spanish Sun'.
• ORIGIN Kordes, Germany, 1974.
• OTHER NAMES 'Friesia', 'Sunsprite'.

☼ ◊

Z 5–9

HEIGHT
2½ft (75cm)

SPREAD
2ft (60cm)

Hybrid Tea (Large-flowered bush)	

ROSA 'Simba'

Habit Upright, neat, free-flowering. **Flowers** Double, urn-shaped, opening rounded, 3½in (9cm) across, strong-stemmed. Clear yellow. **Scent** Light, sweet, and fresh. **Leaves** Large, semi-glossy. Mid-green. **Blooming period** From summer to autumn.
• TIPS Healthy and weather resistant. Good for cutting; useful for beds and borders.
• PARENTAGE 'Korgold' x seedling.
• ORIGIN Kordes, Germany, 1981.
• OTHER NAMES 'Korbelma', 'Goldsmith', 'Helmut Schmidt'.

☼ ◊

Z 5–9

HEIGHT
2½ft (75cm)

SPREAD
2ft (60cm)

Hybrid Tea (Large-flowered bush)	

ROSA 'The Lady'

Habit Upright, open, free-branching. **Flowers** Double, pointed, 4–6in (10–15cm) across, with outer petals reflexing to form a point. Warm yellow, flushed salmon-pink. **Scent** Moderately sweet. **Leaves** Glossy. Mid-green. **Blooming period** Throughout summer and autumn.
• TIPS Good for cutting, exhibition, borders, or tubs. Robust and easily grown. Weather resistant.
• PARENTAGE 'Pink Parfait' x 'Redgold'
• ORIGIN Fryer, England, 1985.
• OTHER NAMES 'Fryjingo'

☼ ◊

Z 5–9

HEIGHT
3ft (90cm)

SPREAD
2ft (60cm)

Floribunda (Cluster-flowered bush or shrub)	

ROSA 'Mountbatten'

Habit Upright, dense. **Flowers** Fully double, rounded, 4in (10cm) across, with neat, round buds, singly, and in clusters. Yellow. **Scent** Sweet. **Leaves** Dark green. **Blooming period** Summer to autumn.
• TIPS Robust and easily grown. Suitable for borders, beds, and hedges. Excellent as a standard. If lightly pruned, will form a specimen shrub.
• PARENTAGE 'Peer Gynt' x [('Anne Cocker' x 'Arthur Bell') x 'Southampton'].
• ORIGIN Harkness, England, 1982.
• OTHER NAMES 'Harmantelle'.

☼ ◊

Z 5–9

HEIGHT
3–5ft
(1–1.5m)
depending
on pruning

SPREAD
32in (80cm)

Floribunda (Cluster-flowered bush)

ROSA 'Allgold'

Habit Sturdy, compact. *Flowers* Rounded, double, 2–4in (5–10cm) across, borne in trusses. Golden-yellow. *Scent* Light but sweet. *Leaves* Glossy. Dark green. *Blooming period* Throughout summer and autumn.
• TIPS Valued for its pure unfading color, this rose is good for cutting and the flowers retain their color well until the petals fall. Although it is a sturdy rose with healthy, disease resistant foliage, it seldom outgrows its allotted space, and has a dainty overall appearance. It is well suited to planting in beds and looks good placed at the front of a border. It responds well to hard pruning, producing new growth freely from the base.
• PARENTAGE 'Goldilocks' x 'Ellinor le Grice'.
• ORIGIN Le Grice, England, 1956.

☼ ◊

Z 5–9

HEIGHT
2–2½ft
(60–70cm)

SPREAD
20in (50cm)

Tea rose	

ROSA 'Lady Hillingdon'

Habit Upright, with slender, arching purplish stems. **Flowers** Nodding, semi-double, cupped, to 6in (15cm) across, in open sprays. Soft apricot-yellow, opening from coppery-apricot buds. **Scent** Rich, fruity, tea-scented. **Leaves** Glossy. Dark green, tinted purple on emergence. **Blooming period** Summer until mid winter in a protected site.
• TIPS Needs a warm, sheltered site and fertile soil. Good for borders, in containers, and under glass.
• PARENTAGE Possibly 'Papa Gontier' x 'Mme. Hoste'.
• ORIGIN Lowe and Shawyer, England, 1910.

☀ ◊

Z 5–9

HEIGHT
2½ft (75cm)

SPREAD
2ft (60cm)

Floribunda (Cluster-flowered bush)	

ROSA 'Harvest Fayre'

Habit Bushy. **Flowers** Double, urn-shaped to rounded, 2½in (6cm) across, borne in neatly spaced clusters. Soft apricot-orange. **Scent** Light, fresh and sweet. **Leaves** Plentiful, glossy. Yellowish-green. **Blooming period** Throughout summer until late autumn.
• TIPS Good for hedging or borders. Performs best if deadheaded regularly.
• PARENTAGE Seedling x 'Bright Smile'.
• ORIGIN Dickson, Northern Ireland, 1990.
• OTHER NAMES 'Dicnorth'.

☀ ◊

Z 5–9

HEIGHT
2½ft (75cm)

SPREAD
2ft (60cm)

Hybrid Tea (Large-flowered bush)	

ROSA 'King's Ransom'

Habit Upright, very floriferous. **Flowers** Double, urn-shaped, opening flat, 5in (12cm) across, with long, strong stems. Rich, unfading, golden-yellow. **Scent** Sweet and fresh, but moderate. **Leaves** Leathery. Dark green. **Blooming period** From summer to autumn.
• TIPS Good for cutting, containers, beds, borders, and hedges.
• PARENTAGE 'Golden Masterpiece' x 'Lydia'.
• ORIGIN Morey, US, 1961.

☀ ◊

Z 5–9

HEIGHT
3ft (90cm)

SPREAD
2ft (60cm)

Hybrid Tea (Large-flowered bush)	

ROSA 'Freedom'

Habit Neat, dense, bushy. **Flowers** Double, rounded, 3½in (9cm) across, freely produced. Clear, bright yellow. **Scent** Moderate. **Leaves** Abundant, glossy. Green. **Blooming period** From summer to autumn.
• TIPS Healthy. Best in its color for a bed of one variety. Responds well to moderate winter pruning.
• PARENTAGE ('Eurorose' x 'Typhoon') x 'Bright Smile'.
• ORIGIN Dickson. Northern Ireland, 1984.
• OTHER NAMES 'Dicjem'.

☀ ◊

Z 5–9

HEIGHT
2½ft (75cm)

SPREAD
2ft (60cm)

Floribunda
(Cluster-flowered bush)

ROSA 'Bright Smile'

Habit Neat, dense, bushy. *Flowers* Flat, semi-double, 3in (8cm) across, opening from neat, slender buds. Butter-yellow. *Scent* Light and sweet. *Leaves* Glossy. Bright green, often faintly flushed red. *Blooming period* From summer to autumn.
• TIPS Good for beds, borders, low hedging, and smaller gardens. Weather resistant.
• PARENTAGE 'Eurorose' x seedling.
• ORIGIN Dickson, Northern Ireland, 1980.
• OTHER NAMES 'Dicdance'.

☼ ◑

Z 5–9

HEIGHT
18in (45cm)

SPREAD
18in (45cm)

Floribunda
(Cluster-flowered bush)

ROSA 'Glenfiddich'

Habit Upright. *Flowers* Double, urn-shaped, 4in (10cm) across, beautifully shaped, borne singly, and in clusters. Rich amber-yellow. *Scent* Sweet and fruity. *Leaves* Glossy. Dark green. *Blooming period* From summer to autumn.
• TIPS Needs a site sheltered from cold winds and hard frosts to perform best. Keep well mulched and free from competition with weeds. Remove dead wood in winter.
• PARENTAGE Seedling x ('Sabine' x 'Circus').
• ORIGIN Cocker, Scotland, 1976.

☼ ◑

Z 5–9

HEIGHT
2½ft (75cm)

SPREAD
2ft (60cm)

Hybrid Tea
(Large-flowered bush)

ROSA 'Pot o' Gold'

Habit Bushy, vigorous, neat, and regular. *Flowers* Fully double, rounded, 3½in (9cm) across, borne singly or in wide, many-flowered sprays. Clear golden-yellow. *Scent* Rich and sweet, fruity. *Leaves* Glossy. Rich green. *Blooming period* Summer to autumn.
• TIPS Excellent for bedding and massed plantings. Good as a standard and for cutting.
• PARENTAGE 'Eurorose' x 'Whisky Mac'.
• ORIGIN Dickson, Northern Ireland, 1980.
• OTHER NAMES 'Dicdivine'.

☼ ◑

Z 5–9

HEIGHT
2½ft (75cm)

SPREAD
2ft (60cm)

Hybrid Tea
(Large-flowered bush)

ROSA 'Warm Wishes'

Habit Upright, open, vigorous, and free-flowering. *Flowers* Double, rounded, 6in (15cm) across. Peachy salmon-pink. *Scent* Strong and sweet. *Leaves* Semi-glossy. Dark green. *Blooming period* From summer to autumn.
• TIPS Excellent for cutting, and good for bedding and borders. May be grown as a standard.
• PARENTAGE 'Pot o' Gold' x (seedling x 'Cheshire Life').
• ORIGIN Fryer, England, 1994.
• OTHER NAMES 'Fryxotic'.

☼ ◑

Z 5–9

HEIGHT
3½ft (1.1m)

SPREAD
28in (70cm)

Hybrid Tea (Large-flowered bush)	

ROSA 'Fulton Mackay'

Habit Vigorous, bushy, upright. *Flowers* Double, urn-shaped, high-centered, 6in (15cm) across. Rich golden-apricot with pink flushes. *Scent* Fresh, moderate. *Leaves* Plentiful, glossy. Dark green. *Blooming period* Throughout summer and autumn.

• TIPS A hardy rose that is easy to grow. The well-formed and nicely scented flowers are excellent for cutting, and a good continuity of bloom can be ensured by regularly deadheading spent flowers. The bushy, upright habit and classically formed, beautifully tinted flowers make this rose especially suitable for geometric beds and borders in a formal rose garden.

• PARENTAGE 'Silver Jubilee' x 'Jana'.
• ORIGIN Cocker, Scotland, 1988.
• OTHER NAMES 'Cocdana'.

☼ ◊

Z 5–9

HEIGHT
2½ft (75cm)

SPREAD
2ft (60cm)

Hybrid Tea
(Large-flowered bush)

ROSA 'Valencia'

Habit Bushy, dense, uneven. *Flowers* Double, rounded, opening from long, elegantly pointed buds, strong-stemmed. Soft, clear amber-gold. *Scent* Strong and sweet. *Leaves* Large, plentiful, glossy. Mid-green. *Blooming period* Summer to autumn.
• TIPS Excellent for cutting, and good for beds and borders. Tolerates light shade. Is best deadheaded after each flush of bloom.
• PARENTAGE Not disclosed.
• ORIGIN Kordes, Germany, 1989.
• OTHER NAMES 'Koreklia'.

☼ ◊

Z 5–9

HEIGHT
3ft (90cm)
or more

SPREAD
2ft (60cm)

Hybrid Tea
(Large-flowered bush)

ROSA 'Princess Royal'

Habit Bushy, upright. *Flowers* Urn-shaped buds opening loosely cupped, double, 4½in (11cm) across. Shades of golden-apricot. *Scent* Light. *Leaves* Semi-glossy. Mid-green. *Blooming period* From summer to autumn.
• TIPS Useful for bedding and borders.
• PARENTAGE 'Tequila Sunrise' x seedling.
• ORIGIN Dickson, Northern Ireland, 1992.
• OTHER NAMES 'Dicroyal'.

☼ ◊

Z 5–9

HEIGHT
32in (80cm)

SPREAD
24in (60cm)

Hybrid Tea
(Large-flowered bush)

ROSA Vidal Sassoon

Habit Bushy, upright, irregular. *Flowers* Double, rounded, to 4in (10cm) across, opening rather flat. Soft buff-lavender. *Scent* Moderately sweet. *Leaves* Plentiful, semi-glossy. Mid-green. *Blooming period* Summer to autumn.
TIPS Excellent for cutting, and useful for borders. Notable for its soft and unusual color.
• PARENTAGE 'Harmonie' x 'Big Purple'.
• ORIGIN McGredy, New Zealand, 1991.
• OTHER NAMES 'Macjuliat', 'Old Spice', 'Spiced Coffee'.

☼ ◊

Z 5–9

HEIGHT
2½ft (75cm)

SPREAD
2ft (60cm)

Hybrid Tea
(Large-flowered bush)

ROSA Peace

Habit Vigorous, shrubby. *Flowers* Fully double, pointed to rounded, 6in (15cm) across. Yellow, pink-flushed. *Scent* Sweet. *Leaves* Plentiful, large, glossy. Bright green. *Blooming period* Summer to autumn.
• TIPS Excellent for beds, borders, hedging, and for cutting and exhibition. Good as a standard.
• PARENTAGE [('George Dickson' x 'Souvenir de Claudius Pernet') x ('Joanna Hill' x 'Charles P. Kilham')] x 'Margaret McGredy'.
• ORIGIN Meilland, France, 1942.
• OTHER NAMES 'Mme A. Meilland', 'Gioia', 'Gloria Dei'.

☼ ◊

Z 5–9

HEIGHT
4ft (1.2m)

SPREAD
3ft (1m)

Hybrid Tea (Large-flowered bush)	

ROSA 'Alpine Sunset'

Habit Compact, upright, vigorous, free-flowering. *Flowers* Rounded, fully double, to 8in (20cm) across, on short stems. Peachy pink, fading to yellow at the petal base. *Scent* Strong and rich. *Leaves* Large, semi-glossy. Mid-green. *Blooming period* Recurrently from summer to autumn.
• TIPS Good for exhibition, borders, and beds. Dies back in hard frosts and cold, dry winds.
• PARENTAGE 'Dr. A.J. Verhage' x 'Grandpa Dickson'.
• ORIGIN Cant, England, 1974.

☼ ◊

Z 5–9

HEIGHT
2ft (60cm)

SPREAD
2ft (60cm)

Hybrid Tea (Large-flowered bush)	

ROSA 'Whisky Mac'

Habit Neat, upright, vigorous, and bushy. *Flowers* Fully double, rounded, to 4½in (11cm) across. Rich golden-amber, suffused with orange. *Scent* Strong and sweetly fruity. *Leaves* Plentiful, glossy. Dark green, red-tinted. *Blooming period* From summer to autumn.
• TIPS Useful for cutting, beds, and borders. Susceptible to mildew and die back in cold winters.
• PARENTAGE Seedling x 'Dr. A.J. Verhage'.
• ORIGIN Tantau, Germany, 1967.
• OTHER NAMES 'Whisky', 'Tanky'.

☼ ◊

Z 5–9

HEIGHT
2½ft (75cm)

SPREAD
2ft (60cm)

Hybrid Tea (Large-flowered bush)	

ROSA 'Indian Summer'

Habit Compact, bushy, irregular. *Flowers* Double, urn-shaped to rounded, 6in (15cm) across. Creamy-apricot-orange. *Scent* Sweet and strong, reminiscent of sweet peas. *Leaves* Plentiful, glossy, rather small. Dark green. *Blooming period* Throughout summer and autumn.
• TIPS Good for cutting, bedding, borders, and containers.
• PARENTAGE Not disclosed.
• ORIGIN Pearce, England, 1991.
• OTHER NAMES 'Peaperfume'.

☼ ◊

Z 5–9

HEIGHT
22in (55cm)

SPREAD
2ft (60cm)

Floribunda (Cluster-flowered bush)	

ROSA 'Champagne Cocktail'

Habit Upright. *Flowers* Cupped, double, 3½in (9cm) across, borne in large, open clusters. Yellow, heavily suffused with pink, with a deeper pink petal reverse. *Scent* Sweet. *Leaves* Dark green. *Blooming period* From summer to autumn.
• TIPS Good for borders and bedding.
• PARENTAGE 'Old Master' x 'Southampton'.
• ORIGIN Horner, England, 1985.
• OTHER NAMES 'Horflash'.

☼ ◊

Z 5–9

HEIGHT
3ft (1m)

SPREAD
2ft (60cm)

Hybrid Tea (Large-flowered bush)

ROSA 'Dawn Chorus'

Habit Upright, neat. **Flowers** Double, pointed, small, 3–4in (7–10cm) across. Deep orange with yellow on petal reverse. **Scent** Faint but sweet. **Leaves** Glossy. Dark green, tinted with red. **Blooming period** Throughout summer to autumn with good continuity.

• TIPS An excellent choice for bedding and for planting in borders. A neat, dense, and shapely bush with glossy, red-tinted foliage that provides an ideal backdrop for the beautifully shaped flowers that open from furled buds.

This versatile rose may also be grown as a standard or in containers. A sturdy and disease-resistant rose.

• PARENTAGE 'Wishing' × 'Peer Gynt'.
• ORIGIN Dickson, Northern Ireland, 1993.
• OTHER NAMES 'Dicquasar'.

☼ ◊

Z 5–9

HEIGHT
2½ft (75cm)

SPREAD
2ft (60cm)

Hybrid Tea (Large-flowered bush)	

ROSA 'Just Joey'

Habit Upright, open, branching. *Flowers* Fully double, rounded, 5in (12cm) across, with slightly serrated petals, opening from long, elegant buds. Coppery-fawn, with buff-pink tints. *Scent* Sweetly and moderately fragrant. *Leaves* Sparse, but attractive, leathery. Dark green. *Blooming period* From summer to autumn.

• TIPS Valued for its unusual coloring, the full-petaled blooms of this rose are excellent for cutting. It is also suitable for beds and borders. A hardy and fairly disease-resistant cultivar, it is easy to grow. If given a warm, sunny site, however, it may produce extremely large blooms that, when fully open, reveal a boss of dark golden stamens.

• PARENTAGE 'Fragrant Cloud' x 'Dr. A.J. Verhage'.

• ORIGIN Cant, England, 1973.

☼ ◊

Z 5–9

HEIGHT
2½ft (75cm)

SPREAD
2ft (60cm)

Floribunda
(Cluster-flowered bush)

ROSA 'Oranges and Lemons'

Habit Upright, bushy, irregular. **Flowers** Double, cupped-rounded, 4in (10cm) across, in large, heavy clusters. Rich golden-yellow, striped, and part-colored scarlet. **Scent** Sweet. **Leaves** Glossy. Dark green, copper-tinted when young. **Blooming period** Summer to autumn.
TIPS Suitable for borders, bedding, and massed plantings. The flower stems bow under the rain
• PARENTAGE 'New Year' x seedling.
• ORIGIN McGredy, Northern Ireland, 1993.
• OTHER NAMES 'Macoranlem'.

Floribunda
(Cluster-flowered bush)

ROSA 'Fragrant Delight'

Habit Bushy, uneven, and irregular. **Flowers** Double, urn-shaped, 3in (8cm) across, in profuse clusters. Pale orange-salmon. **Scent** Moderately strong. **Leaves** Plentiful, glossy. Dark red-tinted, green. **Blooming period** From summer to autumn.
• TIPS Weather resistant. Best in fertile, reliably moisture-retentive soil. Good for borders, hedging, and massed plantings.
• PARENTAGE 'Chanelle' x 'Whisky Mac'.
• ORIGIN Wisbech Plant Co., England, 1978.

☀ ◐

Z 5–9

HEIGHT
32in (80cm)

SPREAD
2ft (60cm)

☀ ◐

Z 5–9

HEIGHT
3ft (1m)

SPREAD
2½ft (75cm)

Floribunda
(Cluster-flowered bush)

ROSA 'Sheila's Perfume'

Habit Upright, vigorous. **Flowers** Double, urn-shaped, 3½in (9cm) across, borne singly, and in clusters. Yellow petals flushed red at the edges. **Scent** Sweet. **Leaves** Glossy. Dark green, red-tinted. **Blooming period** Summer to autumn.
• TIPS Good for cutting, beds, borders, hedging, and containers.
• PARENTAGE 'Peer Gynt' x ['Daily Sketch' x ('Paddy McGredy' x 'Prima Ballerina')]
• ORIGIN Sheridan, England, 1985.
• OTHER NAMES 'Harsherry'.

Hybrid Tea
(Large-flowered bush)

ROSA 'Rosemary Harkness'

Habit Vigorous, spreading. **Flowers** Double, cupped, rounded, 4in (10cm) across, from urn-shaped buds. Orange-yellow, flushed salmon-pink. **Scent** Sweet, like passion fruit. **Leaves** Abundant, glossy. Dark green. **Blooming period** Summer to autumn.
• TIPS Weather resistant. Best in fertile soil, in sun. Good for cutting, borders, hedging, or as a standard.
• PARENTAGE 'Compassion' x ('Basildon Bond' x 'Grandpa Dickson').
• ORIGIN Harkness, England, 1985.
• OTHER NAMES 'Harrowbond'

☀ ◐

Z 5–9

HEIGHT
2½ft (75cm)

SPREAD
2ft (60cm)

☀ ◐

Z 5–9

HEIGHT
32in (80cm)

SPREAD
2½ft (75cm)

Floribunda (Cluster-flowered bush)	

ROSA 'Fellowship'

Habit Bushy, dense, upright. *Flowers* Double, cupped, with center petals infolded, 3–4in (7–10cm) across, borne both in well-spaced clusters and singly. Deep orange. *Scent* Sweet. *Leaves* Abundant, glossy. Dark green. *Blooming period* Throughout summer to autumn.
• TIPS Excellent for bedding and massed plantings. Good for exhibition.
• PARENTAGE 'Southampton' x 'Remember Me'.
• ORIGIN Harkness, England, 1992.
• OTHER NAMES 'Harwelcome', 'Livin' Easy'.

☀ ◐

Z 5–9

HEIGHT
2½ft (75cm)

SPREAD
2ft (60cm)

Hybrid Tea (Large-flowered bush)	

ROSA 'Lover's Meeting'

Habit Vigorous, arching, open. *Flowers* Double, pointed, 4in (10cm) across, with large petals reflexing at the tips to form a point; often borne in large, heavy sprays. Warm reddish-orange, buff-tinted. *Scent* Light and sweet. *Leaves* Plentiful, glossy. Bronze-green. *Blooming period* From summer to autumn.
• TIPS Excellent for cutting, and good for beds and borders. May also be grown as a standard.
• PARENTAGE Seedling x 'Egyptian Treasure'.
• ORIGIN Gandy, England, 1980.

☀ ◐

Z 5–9

HEIGHT
30in (75cm)

SPREAD
30in (75cm)

Floribunda (Cluster-flowered bush)	

ROSA 'Masquerade'

Habit Vigorous, bushy, free-flowering. *Flowers* Semi-double, 2½in (6cm) across, borne in large, sprays. Yellow at first, turning through salmon-pink to red, all colors present at any one time. *Scent* Light. *Leaves* Small, dark green. *Blooming period* Summer to autumn.
• TIPS Generally healthy, and must be deadheaded regularly to ensure continuous flowering.
• PARENTAGE 'Goldilocks' x 'Holiday'.
• ORIGIN Boerner, US, 1949.

☀ ◐

Z 5–9

HEIGHT
3ft (90cm)

SPREAD
2½ft (75cm)

Hybrid Tea (Large-flowered bush)	

ROSA 'Piccadilly'

Habit Vigorous, bushy, upright, and well-branched. *Flowers* Double, pointed, 5in (12cm) across, bright scarlet, with a yellow petal reverse, suffused with orange at maturity. Borne very freely, both singly, and in clusters. *Scent* Light. *Leaves* Abundant, glossy. Dark green, bronze-tinted. *Blooming period* From summer to autumn.
• TIPS Good for beds, borders, hedges, and exhibition. Excellent weather resistance.
• PARENTAGE 'McGredy's Yellow' x 'Karl Herbst'.
• ORIGIN McGredy, Northern Ireland, 1959.

☀ ◐

Z 5–9

HEIGHT
3ft (1m)

SPREAD
2ft (60cm)

Floribunda (Cluster-flowered bush)

ROSA 'Flair'

Habit Compact, bushy. **Flowers** Semi-double, cupped to flat, 2–3in (5–8cm) across, freely borne in well-filled clusters. Rich canary-yellow with red. **Scent** Little. **Leaves** Glossy. Mid-green. **Blooming period** Throughout summer to autumn.

• TIPS A neat, bushy rose that is excellent for the front of a rose bed or border, and particularly suited to a smaller garden where space is at a premium. It is also suitable for containers on patios and other paved or graveled areas in the garden. Valued for its distinctive coloring and compact habit, it has a long and reliable flowering season.

• PARENTAGE 'Sweet Magic' x 'Little Artist'.
• ORIGIN Dickson, Northern Ireland, 1993.
• OTHER NAMES 'Dicrelax'.

☼ ◊

Z 5–9

HEIGHT
18in (45cm)

SPREAD
18in (45cm)

Hybrid Tea
(Large-flowered bush)

ROSA 'Troika'

Habit Vigorous, dense, bushy. *Flowers* Double, pointed, 6in (15cm) across. Orange-yellow, suffused with pink. *Scent* Sweet. *Leaves* Abundant, glossy. Dark green. *Blooming period* From summer to autumn.
- TIPS Excellent for cutting and exhibition, and good for massed plantings.
- PARENTAGE ['Super Star' x ('Baccarà' x 'Princesse Astrid')] x 'Hanne'.
- ORIGIN Poulsen, Denmark, 1972.
- OTHER NAMES 'Royal Dane'.

☼ ◊

Z 5–9

HEIGHT
3ft (1m)

SPREAD
2½ft (75cm)

Hybrid Tea
(Large-flowered bush)

ROSA 'Doris Tysterman'

Habit Vigorous, upright. *Flowers* Pointed, fully double, 4in (10cm) across, freely produced. Rich coppery-orange. *Scent* Faint but sweet. *Leaves* Large, glossy. Dark green. *Blooming period* From summer to autumn.
- TIPS Good for bedding. Rather susceptible to mildew.
- PARENTAGE 'Peer Gynt' x seedling.
- ORIGIN Wisbech Plant Co., England, 1975.

☼ ◊

Z 5–9

HEIGHT
4ft (1.2m)

SPREAD
2½ft (75cm)

Hybrid Tea
(Large-flowered bush)

ROSA 'Remember Me'

Habit Dense, upright, vigorous. *Flowers* Fully double, pointed, 3½in (9cm) across, borne on stiff stems. Deep coppery-orange. *Scent* Light. *Leaves* Abundant, small, glossy. Dark green. *Blooming period* Throughout summer and autumn.
- TIPS Easily grown, but best in a sunny site with shelter from wind. Good for cutting, beds, and hedges. May also be grown as a standard.
- PARENTAGE 'Alexander' x 'Silver Jubilee'.
- ORIGIN Cocker, Scotland, 1984.
- OTHER NAMES 'Cocdestin'.

☼ ◊

Z 5–9

HEIGHT
3ft (1m)

SPREAD
2½ft (75cm)

Hybrid Tea
(Large-flowered bush)

ROSA 'Tequila Sunrise'

Habit Bushy, irregular, robust. *Flowers* Double, rounded, to 4in (10cm) across. Bright golden-yellow, rimmed scarlet-red at the petal edge. *Scent* Light. *Leaves* Glossy. Mid-green. *Blooming period* Throughout summer to autumn.
- TIPS Good for cutting, bedding, hedging, and massed plantings and may be grown as a standard. Needs deadheading to prolong flowering.
- PARENTAGE 'Bonfire Night' x 'Freedom'.
- ORIGIN Dickson, Northern Ireland, 1989.
- OTHER NAMES 'Beaulieu', 'Dicobey'.

☼ ◊

Z 5–9

HEIGHT
2½ft (75cm)

SPREAD
2ft (60cm)

Floribunda
(Cluster-flowered bush)

ROSA 'Southampton'

Habit Upright. *Flowers* Double, pointed, 4in (10cm) across, in clusters. Apricot, flushed with orange and pale scarlet. *Scent* Light, sweet. *Leaves* Glossy. Dark green. *Blooming period* Summer to autumn.
• TIPS Best in a warm, sunny site. Good for bedding, hedging, and containers, and for exhibition.
• PARENTAGE ('Ann Elizabeth' x 'Allgold') x 'Yellow Cushion'
• ORIGIN Harkness, England, 1972.
• OTHER NAMES 'Susan Ann'

☼ ◊

Z 5–9

HEIGHT
3ft (1m)

SPREAD
2ft (60cm)

Floribunda
(Cluster-flowered bush)

ROSA 'Amber Queen'

Habit Spreading. *Flowers* Rounded, fully double, 3–4in (8–10cm) across, in large clusters. Amber-yellow. *Scent* Rich, strong, and heavy. *Leaves* Glossy. Red-tinted, dark green. *Blooming period* Throughout summer and autumn.
• TIPS Good for beds, borders, and low hedging, as well as in containers and for exhibition.
• PARENTAGE 'Southampton' x 'Typhoon'.
• ORIGIN Harkness, England, 1984.
• OTHER NAMES 'Harroony', 'Prinz Eugen van Savoyen'.

☼ ◊

Z 5–9

HEIGHT
20in (50cm)

SPREAD
20in (50cm)

Floribunda
(Cluster-flowered bush)

ROSA 'Anne Harkness'

Habit Upright, vigorous. *Flowers* Urn-shaped, double, 3in (8cm) across, in well-spaced, many-flowered sprays. Rich apricot-yellow. *Scent* Faint, fresh, sweet. *Leaves* Plentiful. Mid-green. *Blooming period* From late summer to autumn.
• TIPS Good for exhibition, cutting, and borders. Responds well to hard pruning.
• PARENTAGE 'Bobby Dazzler' x [('Manx Queen' x 'Prima Ballerina') x ('Chanelle' x 'Piccadilly')].
• ORIGIN Harkness, England, 1980.
• OTHER NAMES 'Harkaramel'.

☼ ◊

Z 5–9

HEIGHT
4ft (1.2m)

SPREAD
2ft (60cm)

Rugosa shrub	

ROSA 'Blanche Double de Coubert'

Habit Dense, bushy. **Flowers** Semi-double, opening flat, 3½in (9cm) across. Pure white, with golden stamens, sometimes pink-flushed in bud. **Scent** Strong, heady, sweet. **Fruits** Large, rounded, red, but not freely produced. **Leaves** Veined, wrinkled. Dark green. **Blooming period** Recurrent, from summer to autumn.
• TIPS Excellent for hedging and borders. Tolerates light shade and most soils and conditions.
• PARENTAGE Possibly *R. rugosa* x 'Sombreuil'.
• ORIGIN Cochet-Cochet, France, 1892.

☀ ◊

Z 3–9

HEIGHT
5ft (1.5m)

SPREAD
4ft (1.2m)

Cluster-flowered shrub	

ROSA 'Penelope'

Habit Dense, bushy, free-flowering. **Flowers** Semi-double, cupped, 3in (8cm) across, borne in large clusters. Pale creamy-blush-pink, fading to white. **Scent** Sweet, musky. **Fruits** Small, coral-pink. **Leaves** Plentiful, large, semi-glossy. Dark green. **Blooming period** Summer to autumn.
• CULTIVATION Excellent for hedging and mixed borders. Remove spent blooms after first flowering to ensure continuity of bloom.
• PARENTAGE 'Ophelia' x unnamed seedling.
• ORIGIN Pemberton, England, 1924.

☀ ◊

Z 5–9

HEIGHT
40in (1m)
or more

SPREAD
40in (1m)

Cluster-flowered shrub	

ROSA 'Francine Austin'

Habit Arching, open, free-flowering. **Flowers** Double, pompon-form, 1–2in (2.5–5cm) across, in spectacular, dainty, wiry-stemmed, many-flowered sprays. Pure white. **Scent** Sweet and delicate. **Leaves** Pale green, with long, narrow, pointed leaflets. **Blooming period** From summer to autumn.
• CULTIVATION Excellent to make an informal group or for a border.
• PARENTAGE 'Alister Stella Grey' x 'Ballerina'.
• ORIGIN Austin, England, 1988.
• OTHER NAMES 'Ausram'.

☀ ◊

Z 4–9

HEIGHT
3ft (90cm)

SPREAD
4ft (1.2m)

Cluster-flowered shrub	

ROSA 'Tall Story'

Habit Arching, spreading. **Flowers** Semi-double, 2–2.5in (5–6cm) across, opening from neatly furled buds, and borne in graceful clusters. Palest primrose-yellow. **Scent** Sweet. **Leaves** Plentiful. Glossy green. **Blooming period** Summer to autumn.
• TIPS Is good for exhibition, ground cover, and borders. May also be grown in containers.
• PARENTAGE 'Korresia' x 'Yesterday'.
• ORIGIN Dickson, Northern Ireland, 1984.
• OTHER NAMES 'Dickooky'.

☀ ◊

Z 5–9

HEIGHT
2½ft (75cm)

SPREAD
4ft (1.2m)

Cluster-flowered shrub	

ROSA 'Many Happy Returns'

Habit Neat, spreading. *Flowers* Semi-double, slightly cupped, 4–5in (10 13cm) across, opening from slender, pointed buds in showy clusters. Blush-pink. *Scent* Moderately sweet. *Leaves* Glossy, dark green. *Blooming period* Throughout summer and autumn.
• TIPS Excellent for mixed borders, beds, massed plantings, and hedging. Needs moderate pruning with the occasional removal of old flower stems to encourage new growth from the base. A healthy and very hardy rose, noted for its long season of bloom.

Its dark, glossy, and very handsome leaves provide a perfect foil for the beautifully formed flowers that are usually borne prolifically. Owing to its name, it is frequently recommended for plantings to commemorate birthdays.
• PARENTAGE 'Herbstfeuer' x 'Pearl Drift'.
• ORIGIN Harkness, England, 1991.
• OTHER NAMES 'Harwanted', 'Prima'.

☼ ◊

Z 5–9

HEIGHT
2½ft (75cm)

SPREAD
2½ft (75cm)

Scotch / Pimpinellifolia hybrid shrub	

ROSA 'Frühlingsmorgen'

Habit Open, well-branched. *Flowers* Single, cupped, 5in (12cm) across. Ivory-white, shading to pink at the petal edge, with golden-brown stamens. *Scent* Hay-scented. *Leaves* Dark grayish-green. *Blooming period* In late spring.
• TIPS Suitable for borders and hedging. Tolerates less fertile soils and light shade.
• PARENTAGE ('E.G. Hill' x 'Cathrine Kordes') x *R pimpinellifolia* 'Altaica'.
• ORIGIN Kordes, Germany, 1941.
• OTHER NAMES 'Spring Morning'.

☼ ◊
___
Z 5–9
___
HEIGHT
to 6ft (2m)
___
SPREAD
5ft (1.5m)

Large-flowered shrub	

ROSA 'Heritage'

Habit Bushy, upright, lax until well-established. *Flowers* Fully double, cupped, 4in (10cm) across, borne in small sprays. Soft apricot-flushed pink. *Scent* Strong, with fresh lemony notes. *Leaves* Semi-glossy, dark green. *Blooming period* Repeating from summer to autumn.
• TIPS Performs best in fertile, well-mulched soils. Suitable for borders.
• PARENTAGE Seedling x ('Wife of Bath' x 'Iceberg').
• ORIGIN Austin, England, 1984.
• OTHER NAMES 'Ausblush'.

☼ ◊
___
Z 5–9
___
HEIGHT
4ft (1.2m)
___
SPREAD
4ft (1.2m)

Large-flowered shrub	

ROSA 'Sweet Juliet'

Habit Vigorous, bushy. *Flowers* Double, shallowly cupped, 4in (10cm) across. Light apricot-yellow. *Scent* Sweetly tea-scented. *Leaves* Plentiful, glossy. Mid-green. *Blooming period* Summer to autumn.
• TIPS Excellent for cutting and mixed borders. Prefers fertile, well-mulched soil.
• PARENTAGE 'Graham Thomas' x 'Admired Miranda'.
• ORIGIN Austin, England, 1989.
• OTHER NAMES 'Ausleap'.

☼ ◊
___
Z 5–9
___
HEIGHT
4ft (1.2m)
___
SPREAD
3ft (90cm)

Species hybrid shrub	

ROSA 'Nevada'

Habit Dense, arching, vigorous. *Flowers* Semi-double, flat, 4in (10cm) across. Creamy-white, pink-flushed in warm weather, with golden stamens. *Scent* Light, delicate. *Leaves* Semi-glossy, light green, with reddish stems. *Blooming period* Early summer, continuing sparsely to autumn.
• TIPS Tolerant of light shade and less-fertile soils. Prune only to remove spent branches.
• PARENTAGE Possibly 'La Giralda' x *R. moyesii* or *R. pimpinellifolia*.
• ORIGIN Dot, Spain, 1927.

☼ ◊
___
Z 5–9
___
HEIGHT
7–10ft
(2.2–3m)
___
SPREAD
7–10ft
(2.2–3m)

Cluster-flowered shrub

ROSA 'Pearl Drift'

Habit Bushy, spreading. **Flowers** Double, cupped, 4in (10cm) or more across, borne in large clusters. Blush-pink. **Scent** Sweet, moderate. **Leaves** Plentiful, glossy. Dark green. **Blooming period** Summer to autumn.
* TIPS Good for mixed borders, beds, and hedging.
* PARENTAGE 'Mermaid' x 'New Dawn'.
* ORIGIN Le Grice, England, 1980.
* OTHER NAMES 'Leggab'.

☀ ◌

Z 5–9

HEIGHT
40in (1m)

SPREAD
4ft (1.2m)

Cluster-flowered shrub

ROSA 'Cornelia'

Habit Vigorous, bushy, spreading. **Flowers** Double, rosette, to 2in (5cm) across, borne in many-flowered clusters. Apricot-pink, fading to creamy-pink; autumn flowers are slightly darker. **Scent** Sweet and musky. **Leaves** Plentiful, small. Dark green. **Blooming period** Summer to autumn.
* TIPS Excellent for cutting, against a wall or fence, or in a large border. Healthy, weather-resistant. Tolerant of light shade and less fertile soil.
* PARENTAGE Unknown.
* ORIGIN Pemberton, England, 1925.

☀ ◌

Z 4–9

HEIGHT
5ft (1.5m)

SPREAD
5ft (1.5m)

Polyantha bush or shrub

ROSA 'The Fairy'

Habit Dense, mound-forming. **Flowers** Double, rosette-form, 1in (2.5cm) across, borne in dainty clusters. Pink. **Scent** Very little. **Leaves** Abundant, small, glossy. Mid-green. **Blooming period** Late summer to late autumn.
* TIPS Excellent for bedding, group plantings, for the front of a mixed border, or containers; may also be grown for ground cover. Also good for cutting. Grows bigger if not pruned.
* PARENTAGE 'Paul Crampel' x 'Lady Gay'.
* ORIGIN Bentall, England, 1932.

☀ ◌

Z 4–9

HEIGHT
2ft (60cm)
or more

SPREAD
2ft (60cm)

Large-flowered shrub

ROSA 'Evelyn'

Habit Bushy, rather stiff. **Flowers** Fully double, cupped-rosette, 4in (10cm) across, with satin-textured petals. Apricot and yellow. **Scent** Fruity and sweet. **Leaves** Semi-glossy, dark green. **Blooming period** From summer to autumn.
* TIPS Healthy, disease-resistant. Suitable for beds and mixed flower borders. Best with only light pruning.
* PARENTAGE 'Graham Thomas' x 'Tamora'.
* ORIGIN Austin, England, 1991.
* OTHER NAMES 'Aussaucer'

☀ ◌

Z 4–9

HEIGHT
3½ft (1.1m)

SPREAD
3ft (90cm)

Cluster-flowered shrub	

ROSA 'Westerland'

Habit Vigorous, upright. **Flowers** Double, cupped, 3½in (9cm) across, with scalloped petals, borne in large clusters. Rich apricot, yellow on the petal reverse. **Scent** Sweet, fresh, and fruity. **Leaves** Plentiful, glossy. Mid-green. **Blooming period** Summer to autumn.
- TIPS Suitable for placement at the back of a mixed border, and may also be grown on a pillar.
- PARENTAGE 'Friedrich Wörlein' x 'Circus'
- ORIGIN Kordes, Germany, 1969.
- OTHER NAMES 'Korwest'.

☼ ◊

Z 5–9

HEIGHT
6ft (1.8m)

SPREAD
4ft (1.2m)

Cluster-flowered shrub	

ROSA 'Felicia'

Habit Vigorous, bushy, spreading. **Flowers** Cupped, fully double, 3in (8cm) across, borne in heavy clusters. Light pink, tinted primrose-yellow at the petal base, with golden stamens. **Scent** Sweet and fairly strong. **Leaves** Glossy, mid-green. **Blooming period** Throughout summer into autumn.
- TIPS Excellent for cutting, bedding, hedging, and containers. Tolerates partial shade.
- PARENTAGE 'Trier' x 'Ophelia'.
- ORIGIN Pemberton, England, 1928.

☼ ◊

Z 4–9

HEIGHT
5ft (1.5m)

SPREAD
7ft (2.2m)

Polyantha shrub	

ROSA 'Ballerina'

Habit Neat, dense, compact. **Flowers** Single, cupped, 1–2in (2.5–5cm) across, in dense, many-flowered clusters. Soft pink with a white center and paler pink petal reverse. **Scent** Light. **Fruits** Small, orange hips. **Leaves** Plentiful, small. Mid-green. **Blooming period** Profusely throughout summer.
- TIPS Good for cutting, exhibition, hedging, mixed borders, massed plantings, and containers. Tolerates light shade and less-fertile soil.
- PARENTAGE Unknown.
- ORIGIN Bentall, England, 1937.

☼ ◊

Z 4–9

HEIGHT
3–4ft
(1–1.2m)

SPREAD
4ft (1.2m)

Cluster-flowered shrub

ROSA 'Octavia Hill'

Habit Vigorous, free-flowering. *Flowers* Double, quartered, 3in (8cm) across, in large, neatly spaced sprays. Clear rose-pink. *Scent* Sweet and fresh. *Leaves* Plentiful, glossy. Dark green. *Blooming period* Summer to autumn.
• TIPS Excellent for mixed borders, especially among old garden roses, and for beds, hedges, standards, and to cut. Prune moderately. Remove old spent stems to promote new growth.
• PARENTAGE 'Armada' x 'Cornelia'.
• ORIGIN Harkness, England, 1995.

☼ ◊

Z 5–9

HEIGHT
6ft (2m)

SPREAD
5ft (1.5m)

Rugosa shrub

ROSA 'Pink Grootendorst'

Habit Upright, bushy, free-flowering. *Flowers* Double, rosette-form, 2in (5cm) across, borne in sprays. Clear pink with serrated petals. *Scent* None. *Leaves* Small, plentiful, leathery. Dark green. *Blooming period* Recurrently from summer to autumn.
• TIPS Good for hedging, mixed borders, and for cutting. Tolerates light shade and hard pruning.
• PARENTAGE Sport of 'F.J. Grootendorst'.
• ORIGIN Grootendorst, The Netherlands, 1923.

☼ ◊

Z 5–9

HEIGHT
3–4ft
(1–1.2m)

SPREAD
3–4ft
(1–1.2m)

Cluster-flowered shrub

ROSA 'Rosy Cushion'

Habit Dense, spreading. *Flowers* Semi-double, cupped, 2½in (6cm) across, in large clusters. Blush-pink fading to ivory-white at the center, with golden stamens. *Scent* Sweet. *Leaves* Plentiful, glossy. Dark green. *Blooming period* Summer to autumn.
• TIPS Superb for borders, hedging, or massed plantings. Deadhead, and prune moderately. Remove flowered stems to promote basal growth.
• PARENTAGE 'Yesterday' x seedling.
• ORIGIN Ilsink, The Netherlands, 1979
• OTHER NAMES 'Interall'.

☼ ◊

Z 5–9

HEIGHT
40in (1m)

SPREAD
4ft (1.2m)

Cluster-flowered shrub

ROSA 'Bonica '82'

Habit Bushy, spreading, vigorous. *Flowers* Fully double, cupped, 3in (8cm) across, in large clusters. Soft rose-pink. *Scent* Sweet, light, delicate. *Leaves* Plentiful, small, glossy. Dark green. *Blooming period* Throughout summer and autumn.
• TIPS Excellent for cutting, bedding, as ground cover, for containers, and as a standard.
• PARENTAGE Probably (*R. sempervirens* x 'Mlle Marthe Carron') x 'Picasso'.
• ORIGIN Meilland, France, 1981.
• OTHER NAMES 'Meidomonac'.

☼ ◊

Z 4–9

HEIGHT
3–4ft
(90cm–
1.2m)

SPREAD
3½–4ft
(1.1–1.2m)

Rugosa shrub	

ROSA 'The Seckford Rose'

Habit Upright, dense. *Flowers* Semi-double, shallowly cupped, 4½in (1cm) across. Rose-pink, with a white eye and golden stamens, aging to blush-pink. *Scent* Sweet and pleasing. *Leaves* Plentiful, veined, and wrinkled. Dark green. *Blooming period* Mainly in summer, but recurrent until autumn.

• TIPS This hardy and healthy rose, along with many other Rugosa roses, is one of the easiest roses to grow. Its upright habit and dense, plentiful foliage make it an excellent choice for hedging, where it will form a prickly and impenetrable barrier. The dark, wrinkled foliage provides a good foil for the fragrant, soft pink flowers.

• PARENTAGE ('Zitronenfalter' x 'Cläre Grammerstorf') x 'Robusta'.

• ORIGIN Kordes, Germany, 1986.

• OTHER NAMES 'Korpinrob', 'Pink Robusta'.

☼ ◌

Z 3–9

HEIGHT
6ft (1.8m)

SPREAD
40in (1m)

| Large-flowered shrub /
climber	

ROSA 'Constance Spry'

Habit Very vigorous, sprawling. *Flowers* Fully double, cupped, 5in (12cm) across. Rich rose-pink. *Scent* Spicy, like myrrh. *Leaves* Plentiful, rather coarse. Grayish-green. *Blooming period* Once in midsummer.
• TIPS Can climb to 12ft (4m) or more and needs support and hard pruning when grown as a shrub. Suitable for a pillar. Tolerates light shade, but needs moderately fertile soil.
• PARENTAGE 'Belle Isis' x 'Dainty Maid'.
• ORIGIN Austin, England, 1961.

☼ ◗

Z 5–9

HEIGHT
6ft (2m)

SPREAD
5ft (1.5m)

Rugosa shrub	

ROSA 'Fru Dagmar Hastrup'

Habit Shrubby, compact. *Flowers* Single, slightly cupped, 4in (10cm) across. Light pink, with creamy-gold stamens. *Scent* Strong, clove-like. *Fruits* Large, round, tomato-red. *Leaves* Glossy, veined, and wrinkled. Light green, red in autumn. *Blooming period* Midsummer, with a lesser flush in autumn.
• TIPS Good for ground cover and low hedging. Tolerates light shade and exposure.
• PARENTAGE Unknown.
• ORIGIN Hastrup, Denmark, 1914.
• OTHER NAMES 'Frau Dagmar Hartopp'.

☼ ◗

Z 3–9

HEIGHT
3ft (90cm)

SPREAD
4ft (1.2m)

Polyantha shrub	

ROSA 'Yesterday'

Habit Bushy, arching. *Flowers* Semi-double, cupped, 1–2in (2.5–5cm) across, in large sprays. Lilac-pink to rosy-violet, with golden stamens. *Scent* Sweet and enduring. *Leaves* Small, shiny. Dark green. *Blooming period* Summer to autumn.
• TIPS Good for hedging, bedding, mixed borders, and containers.
• PARENTAGE ('Phyllis Bide' x 'Shepherd's Delight') x 'Ballerina'.
• ORIGIN Harkness, England, 1974.
• OTHER NAMES 'Tapis d'Orient'.

☼ ◗

Z 4–9

HEIGHT
40in (1m)
or more

SPREAD
40in (1m)

Large-flowered shrub	

ROSA 'Mary Rose'

Habit Vigorous, bushy, spreading. *Flowers* Fully double, cupped, 4–5in (10–13cm) across. Rose-pink, darkening with age; autumn blooms may be paler. *Scent* Sweetly fragrant. *Leaves* Semi-glossy, mid-green. *Blooming period* Early summer to autumn.
• TIPS Excellent for massed plantings and mixed borders. Disease-resistant, and tolerant of a wide range of growing conditions.
• PARENTAGE 'Wife of Bath' x 'The Miller'.
• ORIGIN Austin, England, 1983
• OTHER NAMES 'Ausmary'.

☼ ◗

Z 5–9

HEIGHT
4ft (1.2m)

SPREAD
4ft (1.2m)

Large-flowered shrub	

ROSA 'Gertrude Jekyll'

Habit Open, rather lanky. **Flowers** Fully double, cupped-rosette, 4½in (11cm) across, with folded petals spiraling from the center. Clear deep pink. **Scent** Exceptionally strong and sweet. **Leaves** Thick, mid-green. **Blooming period** Through summer and autumn.
• TIPS Best on fertile, well-mulched soil. Good for cutting and mixed borders.
• PARENTAGE 'Wife of Bath' x 'Comte de Chambord'.
• ORIGIN Austin, England, 1986.
• OTHER NAMES 'Ausbord'

Polyantha shrub	

ROSA 'Marjorie Fair'

Habit Dense, shrubby. **Flowers** Single, slightly cupped, 2in (5cm) across, borne in many-flowered clusters. Deep carmine-red with a white eye. **Scent** None. **Leaves** Small, glossy. Dark green. **Blooming period** Throughout summer and autumn.
• TIPS Good for borders, hedging, massed plantings, and as a specimen. Prune moderately; cut out flowered stems to promote new basal growth.
• PARENTAGE 'Ballerina' x 'Baby Faurax'.
• ORIGIN Harkness, England, 1978.
• OTHER NAMES 'Red Ballerina' , 'Red Yesterday'.

☼ ◊

Z 5–9

HEIGHT
5ft (1.5m)

SPREAD
3ft (90cm)

☼ ◊

Z 4–9

HEIGHT
4ft (1.2m)

SPREAD
4ft (1.2m)

Cluster-flowered shrub	

ROSA 'La Sevillana'

Habit Dense, bushy, leafing well to the ground. **Flowers** Double, cupped, 3in (8cm) across, borne in large trusses. Brilliant red. **Scent** Light. **Leaves** Plentiful, glossy. Bronze-tinted, dark green. **Blooming period** Throughout summer.
• TIPS Excellent for hedging and bedding.
• PARENTAGE [('Meibrim' x 'Jolie Madam') x ('Zambra' x 'Zambra')] x [('Super Star' x 'Super Star') x ('Poppy Flash' x 'Poppy Flash')].
• ORIGIN Meilland, France, 1982.
• OTHER NAMES 'Meigekanu'.

 ☼ ◊

Z 5–9

HEIGHT
4ft (1.2m)

SPREAD
40in (1m)

Cluster-flowered shrub	

ROSA 'Cerise Bouquet'

Habit Very vigorous, arching, majestic. **Flowers** Semi-double, opening flat, 2–3in (5–8cm) across, in open clusters on long stems. Crimson-cerise, with golden stamens, opening from scrolled buds. **Scent** Fruity. **Leaves** Small but plentiful. Gray-green. **Blooming period** Once, in midsummer.
• TIPS Excellent for shrub and mixed borders and will climb to 15ft (5m) with support. May take time to establish well.
• PARENTAGE R. multibracteata x 'Crimson Glory'.
• ORIGIN Tantau, Germany, 1958.

Floribunda / Cluster-flowered shrub	

ROSA 'Eye Paint'

Habit Vigorous, shrubby, dense. **Flowers** Single, opening flat, 2in (5cm) across, in big, well-filled clusters. Bright scarlet with a white eye and golden stamens. **Scent** Light, delicate. **Leaves** Plentiful. Dark green. **Blooming period** Summer to autumn.
• TIPS Hardy, weather-resistant. Good for borders and hedging. Cut blooms to encourage flowering.
• PARENTAGE Seedling x 'Picasso'
• ORIGIN McGredy, New Zealand, 1975.
• OTHER NAMES 'Eyepaint', 'Tapis Persan', 'Maceye'.

☼ ◊

Z 4–9

HEIGHT
11ft (3.5m)

SPREAD
11ft (3.5m)

☼ ◊

Z 5–9

HEIGHT
40in (1m)

SPREAD
2½ft (75cm)

Cluster-flowered shrub	

ROSA 'Cardinal Hume'

Habit Dense, spreading. **Flowers** Double, cupped, 3in (7.5cm) across, borne in dense clusters. Rich crimson-purple, aging to deeper shades. **Scent** Light, fruity, slightly musky. **Leaves** Matte. Dark green. **Blooming period** From summer into autumn.
• TIPS Good for bedding and borders. Prune moderately hard, and occasionally remove old spent stems to promote new growth from the base.
• PARENTAGE Seedling x 'Frank Naylor'.
• ORIGIN Harkness, England, 1984.
• OTHER NAMES 'Harregale'.

☼ ◊

Z 4–9

HEIGHT
40in (1m)

SPREAD
3½ft (1.1m)

Large-flowered shrub	

ROSA 'L. D. Braithwaite'

Habit Bushy, spreading, free-flowering. ***Flowers*** Double, cupped, to 6in (15cm) across. Rich, bright crimson, tending to fade slightly as it ages. ***Scent*** Rich and fruity. ***Leaves*** Dark grayish-green. ***Blooming period*** Summer to autumn.
• TIPS A very hardy, healthy, and vigorous rose that successfully combines the best features of its parents. It is excellent for a shrub or mixed border and, when well grown, repeats reliably and is seldom without flowers during summer and autumn. This rose is particularly valued for its

strong fragrance and the intense, scarcely fading color of its blooms that is displayed to fine effect against the dark foliage. The flowers are good for cutting and arranging, when the scent can be appreciated at close quarters.
• PARENTAGE 'The Squire' x 'Mary Rose'.
• ORIGIN Austin, England, 1988.
• OTHER NAMES 'Auscrim'.

☼ ◊

Z 5–9

HEIGHT
3ft (90cm)

SPREAD
4ft (1.2m)

Rugosa shrub	

ROSA 'Roseraie de l'Haÿ'

Habit Vigorous, dense, bushy. *Flowers* Double, cupped, opening flat, 4½in (11cm) across, velvety. Crimson-purple. *Scent* Strong, heavy, and sweet. *Fruits* Red, rounded, not freely produced. *Leaves* Leathery, wrinkled. Bright green, turning red in autumn. *Blooming period* All summer into autumn.
• TIPS Excellent for hedging; its strong color needs careful placement in mixed borders. Weather-resistant, and tolerates light shade.
• PARENTAGE Sport of *R. rugosa.*
• ORIGIN Cochet-Cochet, France, 1901.

☼ ◊

Z 3–9

HEIGHT
7ft (2.2m)

SPREAD
6ft (2m)

China Rose	

ROSA 'Viridiflora'

Habit Bushy, open, upright, and twiggy. *Flowers* Double, 1in (2.5cm) across, long-lasting. Petals are replaced with serrated green sepals turning purplish with age. *Scent* None. *Leaves* Glossy, dark green, small, pointed. *Blooming period* Summer to autumn.
• TIPS Curious flowers are good for cutting. Best on fertile soil, in full sun, with minimal pruning.
• PARENTAGE Unknown
• ORIGIN Seen growing in S. Carolina, US by 1833.
• OTHER NAMES *R. chinensis* 'Viridiflora', *R. chinensis* var. *viridiflora, R. monstrosa,* 'Green Rose', 'Lü E'.

☼ ◊

Z 7–9

HEIGHT
2½–3ft
(75–90cm)

SPREAD
2ft (60cm)

Cluster-flowered shrub	

ROSA 'Fiona'

Habit Bushy, dense, spreading. *Flowers* Double, opening flat, 2–3in (5–8cm) across, borne in profuse clusters. Blood-red with a white eye and golden stamens. *Scent* Little. *Leaves* Plentiful, small, glossy. Dark green. *Blooming period* Summer to autumn.
• TIPS Excellent for beds, mixed borders, low hedging, or ground cover. Best in a warm, sunny site.
• PARENTAGE 'Sea Foam' x 'Picasso'
• ORIGIN Meilland, France, 1979.
• OTHER NAMES 'Meibeluxen'.

☼ ◊

Z 4–9

HEIGHT
32in (80cm)

SPREAD
4ft (1.2m)

Cluster-flowered shrub	

ROSA 'Jacqueline du Pré'

Habit Vigorous, arching. *Flowers* Semi-double, cupped, 4in (10cm) across. Ivory-white, flushed blush-pink, with scalloped petals and a boss of red-gold stamens. *Scent* Sweet and musky. *Leaves* Glossy, dark green. *Blooming period* Repeating from early summer to autumn.
• TIPS Good for borders, hedging, massed planting, or against a wall. Does best in moist soil.
• PARENTAGE 'Radox Bouquet' x 'Maigold'.
• ORIGIN Harkness, England, 1989.
• OTHER NAMES 'Harwanna'.

☼ ◊

Z 4–9

HEIGHT
6ft (2m)

SPREAD
5ft (1.5m)

Cluster-flowered shrub	

ROSA 'Buff Beauty'

Habit Arching, spreading, leafy. *Flowers* Fully double, cupped, 3½in (9cm) across, in large clusters. Rich apricot to creamy-buff, *Scent* Refreshing and sharp. *Leaves* Large, thick. Dark green. *Blooming period* Recurrently in summer, less often in autumn.
• TIPS Excellent for shrub and mixed borders, and good for cutting. Tolerates light shade and less-fertile soils.
• PARENTAGE Probably a seedling of 'William Allen Richardson'
• ORIGIN Bentall, England, 1939, possibly earlier.

☼ ◊

Z 4–9

HEIGHT
to 5ft
(1.5m)

SPREAD
to 5ft
(1.5m)

Large-flowered shrub	

ROSA 'Golden Wings'

Habit Bushy, spreading. *Flowers* Single, cupped, up to 5in (12cm) across. Clear yellow, with a prominent boss of golden-brown stamens. *Scent* Light and delicately sweet. *Leaves* Glossy, light green. *Blooming period* Throughout summer.
• TIPS Good for hedging. Tolerates less-fertile soils and light shade.
• PARENTAGE ('Soeur Thérèse' × *R. pimpinellifolia* 'Altaica') × 'Ormiston Roy'.
• ORIGIN Shepherd, US, 1956.

☼ ◊

Z 5–9

HEIGHT
3½ft (1.1m)

SPREAD
4½ft
(1.35m)

Rugosa shrub	

ROSA 'Yellow Dagmar Hastrup'

Habit Bushy, spreading. *Flowers* Double, loosely formed, slightly cupped, 4–6in (10–15cm) across. Yellow, with creamy-gold stamens. *Scent* Moderately strong and fruity. *Leaves* Matte, wrinkled. Mid-green. *Blooming period* Mainly in midsummer, with lesser flushes until autumn.
• TIPS Suitable for ground cover.
PARENTAGE 'Golden Angel' × 'Belle Poitevine'
• ORIGIN Moore, US, 1987.
• OTHER NAMES 'Moryelrug', 'Rustica 91', 'Topaz Jewel'.

☼ ◊

Z 3–9

HEIGHT
32in (80cm)

SPREAD
36in (90cm)

Cluster-flowered shrub	

ROSA 'Sally Holmes'

Habit Narrowly upright. *Flowers* Single, cupped, 4–6in (10–5cm) across, borne in very large clusters on lofty stems. Ivory-white to creamy-buff. *Scent* Sweet and delicate. *Leaves* Large, glossy. Dark green. *Blooming period* Repeating throughout summer and into autumn.

• TIPS Good for bedding and borders, although its narrow and strongly upright habit needs careful placement. In this rose, the large, heavy flower clusters can sometimes give a rather top-heavy effect on such a narrowly upright bush. To remedy this, some growers recommend the removal of the topmost flower clusters, early in the season, to encourage branching lower down; the flower clusters that are borne on side branches are far more delicate and open in appearance.

• PARENTAGE 'Ivory Fashion' x 'Ballerina'.

• ORIGIN Holmes, England, 1976.

☼ ◊

Z 5–9

HEIGHT
6ft (1.8m)

SPREAD
3ft (90cm)

Scotch / Pimpinellifolia hybrid shrub	

ROSA 'Frühlingsgold'

Habit Vigorous, arching, tree-like, with downy red-gold thorns on young shoots. **Flowers** Semi-double, cupped, opening flat, to 6in (15cm) across. Primrose yellow, with golden stamens. **Scent** Vanilla-like. **Leaves** Small, abundant. Mid-green. **Blooming period** Early summer.
• TIPS Good for borders and as a specimen.
• PARENTAGE 'Joanna Hill' x R. pimpinellifolia 'Hispida'
• ORIGIN Kordes, Germany, 1937.
• OTHER NAMES 'Spring Gold'.

☼ ◊

Z 5–9

HEIGHT
to 8ft
(2.5m)

SPREAD
7ft (2.2m)

Cluster-flowered shrub	

ROSA 'Chinatown'

Habit Vigorous, bushy, irregular. **Flowers** Fully double, rounded, 4in (10cm) across, in clusters. Deep yellow, sometimes flushed pink. **Scent** Sweet, strong. **Leaves** Plentiful, glossy. Dark green. **Blooming period** All summer, into autumn.
• TIPS Good for bedding, borders, and hedging. May be grown as an espalier and will climb with support. Needs light pruning.
• PARENTAGE 'Columbine' x 'Cläre Grammerstorf'
• ORIGIN Poulsen, Denmark, 1963.
• OTHER NAMES 'Ville de Chine'.

☼ ◊

Z 4–9

HEIGHT
4ft (1.2m)
or more

SPREAD
3ft (90cm)

Large-flowered shrub	

ROSA 'The Pilgrim'

Habit Vigorous, bushy, upright. **Flowers** Fully double, cupped, opening flat, 4½in (11cm) across. Pure yellow, with soft-textured petals. **Scent** Strong, sweet. **Leaves** Plentiful. Dark green. **Blooming period** From summer to autumn.
• TIPS Strong, healthy, and disease-resistant. Good for cutting and mixed borders.
• PARENTAGE ' Graham Thomas' x 'Yellow Buttons'.
• ORIGIN Austin, England, 1991.
• OTHER NAMES 'Auswalker'.

☼ ◊

Z 5–9

HEIGHT
3½ft (1.1m)

SPREAD
3½ft (1.1m)

Large-flowered shrub	

ROSA 'English Garden'

Habit Upright, compact. **Flowers** Double, bowl-shaped, quartered, and opening flat, 3½–6in (9–15cm) across. Ivory-white, flushed buff at center. **Scent** Tea-scented. **Leaves** Plentiful, light green. **Blooming period** Summer to autumn.
• TIPS Prefers fertile, well-mulched soil. Prune lightly to keep compact.
• PARENTAGE ('Lilian Austin' x seedling) x ('Iceberg' x 'Wife of Bath').
• ORIGIN Austin, England, 1987.
• OTHER NAMES 'Ausbuff'.

Large-flowered shrub	

ROSA 'Graham Thomas'

Habit Vigorous, bushy, arching. **Flowers** Fully double, deeply cupped, 4½in (11cm) across. Warm, deep yellow. **Scent** Sweet, tea-scented. **Leaves** Smooth, glossy. Mid-green. **Blooming period** From early summer to autumn.
• TIPS Good for cutting, mixed borders, also as a standard. Deadhead to prolong flowering.
• PARENTAGE 'Charles Austin' x ('Iceberg' x seedling).
• ORIGIN Austin, England, 1983.
• OTHER NAMES 'Ausmas'.

☼ ◊

Z 5–9

HEIGHT
3ft (90cm)

SPREAD
2½ft (75cm)

☼ ◊

Z 5–9

HEIGHT
4ft (1.2m)

SPREAD
5ft (1.5m)

Persica hybrid shrub	

ROSA 'Euphrates'

Habit Sprawling, bushy, hummock-forming. **Flowers** Single, cupped, to 2in (5cm) across, borne in clusters. Five salmon-pink petals, each with a scarlet basal blotch. **Scent** Unscented. **Leaves** Bluish-green, with serrated, variably shaped leaflets. **Blooming period** Once in summer.
• TIPS Disease-resistant; tolerates light shade. Suitable for bedding, borders, and low hedges.
• PARENTAGE R. persica x 'Fairy Changeling'.
• ORIGIN Harkness, England, 1986.
• OTHER NAMES 'Harunique'.

Large-flowered shrub	

ROSA 'Abraham Darby'

Habit Bushy, arching, rounded. **Flowers** Double, deeply cupped, to 6in (15cm) across. Apricot-pink, pale yellow on petal reverse. **Scent** Rich and fruity. **Leaves** Glossy, dark green. **Blooming period** Recurrently throughout summer and autumn.
• TIPS Good in a border or against a wall. Prune as a shrub, or simply remove dead wood for a more natural form.
• PARENTAGE 'Aloha' x 'Yellow Cushion'.
• ORIGIN Austin, England, 1985.
• OTHER NAMES 'Auscot'.

☼ ◊

Z 6–9

HEIGHT
2ft (60cm)

SPREAD
2½ft (75cm)

☼ ◊

Z 5–9

HEIGHT
5ft (1.5m)
or more

SPREAD
5ft (1.5m)

Damask	

ROSA 'Madame Hardy'

Habit Vigorous, upright. **Flowers** Fully double, quartered-rosette, 4in (10cm) across. Pure white with a green button eye. **Scent** Fresh and sweet. **Leaves** Plentiful, matte, leathery. Dark green. **Blooming period** Midsummer.
• TIPS Tolerates light shade and poorer soils. Excellent for a mixed border. Prune after flowering to shape and shorten flowered wood.
• PARENTAGE Unknown.
• ORIGIN Hardy, France, 1832.

☼ ◊

Z 4–9

HEIGHT
5ft (1.5m)

SPREAD
4ft (1.2m)

Species / Wild rose hybrid	DOUBLE SCOTCH ROSE, DOUBLE BURNET ROSE

ROSA PIMPINELLIFOLIA double white

Habit Dense, bushy, very thorny, suckering. **Flowers** Double, cupped, 1½–2in (4–5cm) across, wreathing the stems. Creamy-white. **Scent** Sweet. **Fruits** Small black hips. **Leaves** Small, fern-like, dark green. **Blooming period** Early summer.
• CULTIVATION Excellent for informal hedging, as a specimen, or in a woodland garden. Very healthy.
• PARENTAGE Sport of the species.
• ORIGIN Species occurs in Europe and Asia.
• OTHER NAMES R. pimpinellifolia 'Plena', R. spinosissima 'Plena'.

☼ ◊

Z 5–9

HEIGHT
3ft (1m)

SPREAD
4ft (1.2m)

Bourbon	

ROSA 'Boule de Neige'

Habit Upright, open with arching stems. **Flowers** Fully double, deeply cupped rosette, 3in (8cm) across, reflexing to form a ball, and borne in clusters. Pure white; buds are crimson-tinted. **Scent** Strong, sweet, and heady. **Leaves** Smooth, dark green. **Blooming period** Midsummer with sporadic repeat bloom to autumn.
• CULTIVATION Makes an effective short climber or pillar, if trained on a support. Mulch regularly.
• PARENTAGE 'Blanche Lafitte' x 'Sappho'.
• ORIGIN Lacharme, France, 1867.

☼ ◊

Z 5–9

HEIGHT
5ft (1.5m)

SPREAD
4ft (1.2m)

Bourbon	

ROSA 'Souvenir de la Malmaison'

Habit Bushy, dense, spreading. **Flowers** Fully double, quartered-rosette, 5in (12cm) across. Blush-pink fading to white, with silky petals. **Scent** Sweet, spicy, and heady. **Leaves** Large. Mid-green. **Blooming period** Repeating throughout summer.
• TIPS Tolerates a range of climates, but wet weather makes flowers form soggy "balls". Best in well-mulched soil. Excellent for mixed borders.
• PARENTAGE 'Mme. Desprez' x a Tea Rose.
• ORIGIN Béluze, France, 1843.
• OTHER NAMES 'Queen of Beauty and Fragrance'.

☼ ◊

Z 5–9

HEIGHT
5ft (1.5m)

SPREAD
5ft (1.5m)

Species / Wild rose hybrid	DUPONT ROSE, SNOWBUSH ROSE

ROSA 'Dupontii'

Habit Vigorous, upright, then slightly spreading. **Flowers** Single, flat, 2½in (6cm) across, borne in open sprays. Creamy-white, sometimes pink-flushed, showing yellow stamens. **Scent** Sweet, very fragrant. **Fruits** Orange hips. **Leaves** Slightly downy, grayish-green. **Blooming period** Midsummer, with an occasional later flower.
• TIPS Suitable for hedges, mixed borders, or open glades in a woodland garden. Tolerates poorer soils. This rose provides elegant contrasts between the beautifully formed, creamy-white flowers and the grayish-green foliage. It is thought to have originated at the Empress Josephine's garden at Malmaison, and was illustrated by Redouté as *R. damascena subalba*.
• PARENTAGE Possibly *R. damascena* × *R. moschata*.
• ORIGIN France, before 1817
• OTHER NAMES *R.* × *dupontii*, *R. moschata* var. *nivea*.

☼ ◊

Z 5–9

HEIGHT
7–8ft
(2.2–2.5m)

SPREAD
7ft (2.2m)

China	

ROSA 'Perle d'Or'

Habit Bushy, with slender, twiggy branches.
Flowers Double, urn-shaped, 1½in (4cm) across, in
open, many-flowered clusters. Honey-tinted pink.
Scent Delicate and sweet. *Leaves* Glossy, pointed.
Dark green. *Blooming period* Summer to autumn.
• TIPS Excellent for a mixed border and for cutting.
For cutting and exhibition, it may be grown under
glass in a cool greenhouse.
• PARENTAGE *R. multiflora* seedling x 'Mme. Falcot'.
• ORIGIN Rambaux, int. Dubreuil, France, 1883.
• OTHER NAMES 'Yellow Cécile Brunner'.

☼ ◊

Z 7–9

HEIGHT
4ft (1.2m)
or more

SPREAD
3ft (1m)

Centifolia	

ROSA 'Fantin Latour'

Habit Vigorous, shrubby. *Flowers* Fully double,
cupped, 4in (10cm) across,borne in large clusters.
Clear, deep pink at first, fading quickly to blush-
pink. Outer petals reflex at maturity to reveal a
green button eye. *Scent* Fresh, delicate, and
sweet. *Leaves* Smooth, dark green. *Blooming
period* Midsummer.
• TIPS Excellent for a mixed border. Tolerates
poorer soils but needs an open site.
• PARENTAGE Unknown.
• ORIGIN Uncertain, c. 1900.

☼ ◊

Z 4–9

HEIGHT
5ft (1.5m)

SPREAD
4ft (1.2m)

Scotch	

ROSA 'Stanwell Perpetual'

Habit Dense, twiggy, suckering. *Flowers* Fully
double, opening flat, 3in (8cm) across. Blush-pink,
fading almost to white in warm weather. *Scent*
Sweet, delicate, and pervasive. *Leaves* Small,
neatly toothed. Grayish-green. *Blooming period*
Repeating after the first flush in midsummer.
• TIPS Good for hedging, mixed borders, and as a
specimen. Shape hedges in summer.
• PARENTAGE Possibly *R. pimpinellifolia* x 'Quatre
Saisons' (*R. damascena* 'Semperflorens').
• ORIGIN Lee, England, 1838.

☼ ◊

Z 5–9

HEIGHT
3ft (1m)

SPREAD
4ft (1.2m)

Alba	

ROSA 'Great Maiden's Blush'

Habit Vigorous, upright, arching under the weight
of bloom. *Flowers* Fully double, rosette, 3in (7.5cm)
across, borne in abundance. Light blush-pink, *Scent*
Strong, but sweet and delicate. *Leaves* Bluish-gray.
Blooming period Midsummer.
• TIPS Good for hedging or mixed borders.
Remove some of the older wood after flowering,
and shorten remaining stems. Best if well mulched.
• PARENTAGE Unknown.
• ORIGIN Ancient, maybe 15th century or earlier.
• OTHER NAMES 'Cuisse de Nymphe', 'La Séduisante'.

☼ ◊

Z 4–9

HEIGHT
6ft (2m)

SPREAD
4½ft (1.3m)

China	SWEETHEART ROSE, MALTESE ROSE

ROSA 'Cécile Brünner'

Habit Upright, rather slender, and open. **Flowers** Fully double, urn-shaped, 1½in (4cm) across, opening from scrolled buds, borne singly in large well-spaced clusters. Pale shell-pink. **Scent** Light and fresh. **Leaves** Small, sparse, smooth. Dark green. **Blooming period** From summer to autumn.
• TIPS Suitable for mixed borders, containers, and for buttonholes.
• PARENTAGE A polyantha rose × 'Mme.de Tartas'.
• ORIGIN Veuve Ducher, France, 1880.
• OTHER NAMES 'Mignon', 'Mlle. Cécile Brünner'.

☼ ◊

Z 6–9

HEIGHT
2½ft (75cm)

SPREAD
2ft (60cm)

Species / Wild rose	EGLANTINE, SWEET BRIAR

ROSA EGLANTERIA

Habit Vigorous, arching, thorny. **Flowers** Single, cupped, 1in (2.5cm) across, borne singly, or in small clusters. Pink, with a paler center and golden stamens. **Scent** Light. **Fruits** Oval, scarlet hips. **Leaves** Plentiful, neatly toothed, dark green, apple-scented. **Blooming period** Midsummer.
• TIPS Good for hedging or a woodland garden. Tolerates partial shade and hard clipping.
• ORIGIN Europe to S.W. Asia, often on chalky soils and on downland.
• OTHER NAMES R. rubiginosa.

☼ ◊

Z 5–8

HEIGHT
to 8ft (2.4m)

SPREAD
to 8ft (2.4m)

Alba	

ROSA 'Céleste'

Habit Vigorous, spreading, bushy. **Flowers** Double, cupped, 3in (8cm) across, opening from scrolled buds. Uniform pale pink. **Scent** Very sweetly fragrant. **Fruits** Long, red hips. **Leaves** Gray-green. **Blooming period** In midsummer.
• TIPS Good for hedging and mixed borders. Tolerates light shade. Remove the oldest wood at the base, and shorten stems after flowering.
• PARENTAGE Unknown, possibly The Netherlands.
• ORIGIN Unknown, probably ancient.
• OTHER NAMES 'Celestial'.

☼ ◊

Z 4–9

HEIGHT
5ft (1.5m)

SPREAD
4ft (1.2m)

Centifolia	

ROSA 'Petite de Hollande'

Habit Bushy, compact. **Flowers** Fully double, quartered-rosette, 2in (5cm) across, in profuse clusters. Pink, with darker centers. **Scent** Rich and sweet. **Leaves** Matte, coarsely toothed. Mid-green. **Blooming period** Midsummer.
• TIPS Good for containers and mixed borders. Cut back new growth by half after flowering.
• PARENTAGE Unknown.
• ORIGIN Perhaps The Netherlands, c.1800.
• OTHER NAMES 'Normandica', 'Petite Junon de Hollande', 'Pompon des Dames'.

☼ ◊

Z 4–9

HEIGHT
3ft (1m)

SPREAD
3ft (1m)

Species / Wild rose	

ROSA GLAUCA

Habit Vigorous, arching. *Flowers* Single, flat, 1½in (4cm) across, borne in small, open clusters. Cerise-pink with white centers and golden stamens. *Scent* Little. *Fruits* Small, rounded, dark red, in clusters. *Leaves* Small. Violet-tinted when young, purplish-gray in sun, gray-green in partial shade. *Blooming period* Early summer.
• TIPS Foliage provides contrast in a mixed border or arrangements. Tolerates light shade.
• ORIGIN Mountains of C. Europe.
• OTHER NAMES *R. ferruginea, R. rubrifolia.*

☼ ◊

Z 4–9

HEIGHT
6ft (2m) or more with support

SPREAD
5ft (1.5m)

Bourbon	

ROSA 'Reine Victoria'

Habit Lax, arching, graceful. *Flowers* Fully double, deeply cupped, 3–4in (8–10cm) across, along slender, arching stems. Rose-pink. *Scent* Sweet and heady. *Leaves* Plentiful. Light green. *Blooming period* Repeats from summer to autumn.
• TIPS Excellent as a specimen or for a mixed border. Suitable to grow on a pillar. Provide fertile, well-mulched soil. Prone to blackspot.
• PARENTAGE Unknown.
• ORIGIN Schwartz, France, 1872
• OTHER NAMES 'La Reine Victoria'.

☼ ◊

Z 5–9

HEIGHT
6ft (1.8m)

SPREAD
4ft (1.2m)

Alba	

ROSA 'Königin von Dänemark'

Habit Vigorous, lax, open, thorny. *Flowers* Fully double, quartered-rosette, 3in (8cm) across, warm rose-pink, paling as it opens, with a yellow button eye. *Scent* Rich, strong, and sweet. *Leaves* Coarse. Gray-green. *Blooming period* Midsummer.
• TIPS Good for a mixed border or hedge.
• PARENTAGE Uncertain, possibly an Alba x Damask, or a seedling of 'Maiden's Blush'.
• ORIGIN Booth, Hamburg, 1826.
• OTHER NAMES 'Belle Courtisanne', 'Queen of Denmark'.

☼ ◊

Z 4–9

HEIGHT
5ft (1.5m)

SPREAD
4ft (1.2m)

Moss	

ROSA × *CENTIFOLIA* 'Muscosa'

Habit Lax, open, vigorous. *Flowers* Fully double, rounded-cupped, 3in (8cm) across. Clear pink with a button eye and dense, bright green mossing on calyx, sepals, and stem. *Scent* Sweet, rich, heady. *Leaves* Plentiful, large, coarsely toothed. Mid-green. *Blooming period* Over a long period in midsummer.
• TIPS Prune lightly after flowering.
• PARENTAGE Mutation of *R.* × *centifolia.*
• ORIGIN France, about 1700; the original Moss rose.
• OTHER NAMES 'Communis', 'Old Pink Moss', 'Common Moss'.

☼ ◊

Z 4–9

HEIGHT
5ft (1.5m)

SPREAD
4ft (1.2m)

Damask	

ROSA 'Ispahan'

Habit Vigorous, upright, shrubby. *Flowers* Fully double, cupped, 3in (8cm) across. Warm pink. *Scent* Rich and heady. *Leaves* Plentiful. Gray-green. *Blooming period* Over long periods in summer.
• TIPS Suitable for hedging, mixed borders, and containers. Prune to shape, and remove a proportion of oldest wood after flowering.
• PARENTAGE Unknown.
• ORIGIN Possibly Persian, before 1832.
• OTHER NAMES 'Pompon des Princes', 'Rose d'Isfahan'.

☼ ◊

Z 4–9

HEIGHT
5ft (1.5m)

SPREAD
4ft (1.2m)

Portland	

ROSA 'Marchesa Boccella'

Habit Upright, compact. *Flowers* Fully double, perfectly quartered rosette, to 4½–6in (11–15cm) across. Clear pink, fading paler, with a neat green button eye. *Scent* Rich, sweet, and heady. *Leaves* Plentiful. Light green. *Blooming period* Repeating throughout summer.
• TIPS Sturdy, healthy, but needs fertile, well-mulched soil to perform well.
• PARENTAGE Unknown.
• ORIGIN Moreau-Robert, France, 1868.
• OTHER NAMES 'Jacques Cartier'.

☼ ◊

Z 5–9

HEIGHT
6ft (1.8m)

SPREAD
3ft (90cm)

Species / Wild rose	

ROSA NITIDA

Habit Upright, bushy, suckering. *Flowers* Single, flat, 2in (5cm) across, in great profusion. Bright lilac-rose, with creamy-gold stamens. *Scent* Evening-scented, reminiscent of lily-of-the valley. *Fruits* Rounded, deep scarlet, long-persistent. *Leaves* Small, narrow, shiny. Dark green, turning red and purple in autumn. *Blooming period* Midsummer.
• TIPS Good for containers and ground cover. Best in moist but well-drained, fertile, neutral to acid soil, in an open site.
• ORIGIN N. America, 1807.

☼ ◊

Z 4–9

HEIGHT
2ft (60cm)

SPREAD
3ft (90cm)

Portland	

ROSA 'Madame Knorr'

Habit Vigorous, upright, bushy, free-flowering.
Flowers Fully double, quartered-rosette, 4in (10cm)
across. Rich, clear pink. *Scent* Sweet, pervasive.
Leaves Abundant. Large, gray-green. *Blooming
period* Recurrent, through summer and autumn.
• TIPS Excellent for a smaller garden, and good for
hedging. Tolerant of a wide range of climatic
conditions.
• PARENTAGE Unknown.
• ORIGIN Verdier, France, 1855.
• OTHER NAMES 'Comte de Chambord'.

☀ ◐

Z 5–9

HEIGHT
4ft (1.2m)

SPREAD
3ft (1m)

Hybrid Perpetual	

ROSA 'Mrs John Laing'

Habit Bushy, free-flowering. *Flowers* Fully
double, rounded, 5in (12cm) across, opening
from long-stemmed, pointed buds. Clear
silvery-pink. *Scent* Rich and sweet. *Leaves*
Plentiful. Light green. *Blooming period*
Repeating from summer to autumn.
• TIPS Good for beds, mixed borders,
containers, and excellent for cutting for
arrangements.
• PARENTAGE Seedling of 'François Michelon'.
• ORIGIN Bennett, England, 1887.

☀ ◐

Z 5–9

HEIGHT
3ft (1m)

SPREAD
32in (80cm)

Bourbon	

ROSA 'Variegata di Bologna'

Habit Upright, arching, slender growth. *Flowers*
Fully double, quartered-rosette, 3–4in (8–10cm)
across. Palest blush-pink, striped and splashed
with rose-purple. *Scent* Rich, sweet, and heady.
Leaves Plentiful. Light green. *Blooming period*
Usually in summer, only rarely later.
• TIPS Grow in a warm, sunny, sheltered site, and
provide fertile, well-mulched soil. Prune in winter.
Prone to blackspot. Best with some support.
• PARENTAGE Unknown.
• ORIGIN Bonfiglioli, Italy, 1909.

☀ ◐

Z 5–9

HEIGHT
6ft (2m)

SPREAD
4½ft (1.4m)

China	

ROSA 'Old Blush China'

Habit Bushy, compact, free-flowering, with few
thorns. *Flowers* Double, cupped, 2½in (6cm) across.
Pink, fading silvery-pink. *Scent* Faint, of sweet
peas. *Leaves* Shiny, pointed. Mid-green. *Blooming
period* Almost continuously from summer to winter.
• TIPS May be grown as a climber on a sheltered
wall. Tolerates partial shade.
• PARENTAGE Unknown.
• ORIGIN From China, to Europe, c. 1752.
• OTHER NAMES 'Common Blush China', 'Monthly
Rose', 'Parsons' Pink China'.

☀ ◐

Z 7–9

HEIGHT
3ft (1m) or
more with
support

SPREAD
32in (80cm)
or more

Gallica

Rosa 'Complicata'

Habit Vigorous, arching, very thorny. **Flowers** Single, cupped, 4½–5in (11–12cm) across, opening wide, with pink petals, white at the base, around a boss of golden stamens. **Scent** Light, fresh, and sweet. **Fruits** Globose, orange. **Leaves** Plentiful. Fresh gray-green. **Blooming period** Midsummer.
• TIPS If unsupported, this rose will form a large, gracefully arching shrub and is particularly suited to being grown as informal hedging, in semi-wild, or more naturalistic parts of the garden. Alternatively, if given support, it can be trained to grow through old trees, providing a cascade of color during its blooming period. The flowers, which are borne along the length of the flexible stems, arc particularly attractive to honeybees.
• PARENTAGE Unknown, possibly involves *R. canina* or *R. macrantha.*
• ORIGIN Unknown.

☼ ◊

Z 5–9

HEIGHT
to 7ft
(2.2m)

SPREAD
to 8ft
(2.5m)

Gallica	ROSA MUNDI

ROSA GALLICA 'Versicolor'

Habit Neat, bushy. *Flowers* Semi-double, flat, 2in (5cm) across. Palest blush-pink, striped light red and crimson, with golden-yellow stamens. *Scent* Light and delicate. *Leaves* Matte. Midgreen. *Blooming period* Midsummer.
• TIPS Excellent for mixed borders and hedging. Best on well-mulched soil in an open site. After flowering, reduce new shoots by one-third.
• PARENTAGE Sport of *R.* 'Officinalis'.
• ORIGIN Known since the 16th century.
• OTHER NAMES *R. gallica* 'Variegata'.

☼ ◐

Z 4–9

HEIGHT
2½ft (75cm)

SPREAD
3ft (1m)

China	

ROSA ODORATA 'Mutabilis'

Habit Open, graceful, spindly. *Flowers* Single, shallowly cupped, 2⅓in (6cm) across. Buff-yellow, aging to pink, then slate-purple. *Scent* Little. *Leaves* Plentiful, glossy. Coppery when young. *Blooming period* Early summer to autumn.
• TIPS Good for hedging, containers, or as a climber on a sheltered wall. Avoid exposed sites.
• PARENTAGE Unknown.
• ORIGIN From China, before 1894.
• OTHER NAMES *R. chinensis* 'Mutabilis', 'Mutabilis', 'Tipo Ideale'.

☼ ◐

Z 7–9

HEIGHT
4ft (1.2m)

SPREAD
3ft (90cm)

Gallica	

ROSA 'Charles de Mills'

Habit Upright, arching, almost thornless. *Flowers* Fully double, quartered-rosette, 4–5in (10–13cm) across, opening flat. Rich beetroot-purple, with lilac-gray tones, fading slightly to deep red-purple. *Scent* Moderately strong. *Leaves* Plentiful, matte. Dark green. *Blooming period* Midsummer.
• TIPS Good for hedging; best with some support. Remove old, unproductive stems after flowering.
• PARENTAGE Unknown.
• ORIGIN Unknown.
• OTHER NAMES 'Bizarre Triomphant'.

☼ ◐

Z 5–9

HEIGHT
4ft (1.2m)

SPREAD
3ft (1m)

Bourbon	

ROSA 'Louise Odier'

Habit Upright, arching. *Flowers* Fully double, cupped, camellia-like, 3½–5in (9–12cm) across, in clusters. Warm rose-pink with lilac tones. *Scent* Rich and sweet. *Leaves* Light gray-green. *Blooming period* Repeats from midsummer to autumn.
• TIPS Best with support and on fertile, well-mulched soil. Prune in early spring as a large-flowered bush rose, but much more lightly.
• PARENTAGE Seedling of 'Emile Courtier'.
• ORIGIN Margottin, France, 1851.
• OTHER NAMES 'Mme. de Stella'.

Gallica	APOTHECARY'S ROSE, PROVINS ROSE

ROSA GALLICA var. OFFICINALIS

Habit Neat, bushy, suckering. *Flowers* Semi-double, flat, 3in (8cm) across. Pinkish-red with golden stamens. *Scent* Fresh. *Fruits* Small, round, red hips. *Leaves* Plentiful, rough-textured. Dark green. *Blooming period* Mid- to late summer.
• TIPS Suitable for mixed borders and sunny banks. Apt to sucker readily.
• PARENTAGE The oldest cultivated form of *R. gallica.*
• ORIGIN Known since the 13th century.
• OTHER NAMES 'Red Damask'.

☀ ◐

Z 5–9

HEIGHT
6ft (2m)

SPREAD
4ft (1.2m)

☀ ◐

Z 4–9

HEIGHT
32in (80cm)

SPREAD
36in (1m)

Centifolia	

ROSA × CENTIFOLIA 'Cristata'

Habit Lax, branching, shrubby. *Flowers* Fully double, cupped, 3½in (9cm) across. Rich, clear pink, with an enlarged calyx (resembling a three-cornered hat) clothed in green, moss-like growth. *Scent* Sweet, pervasive. *Leaves* Plentiful, large, drooping. Matte green. *Blooming period* Midsummer.
• TIPS Good supported on a tripod; mulch well.
• PARENTAGE Sport or seedling of *R. × centifolia.*
• ORIGIN Switzerland, 1820.
• OTHER NAMES 'Crested Moss', 'Chapeau de Napoleon', 'Crested Provence'.

Damask	

ROSA 'De Rescht'

Habit Upright, compact. *Flowers* Fully double, camellia-like, 3in (8cm) across, deep mauve-red aging magenta-pink. *Scent* Strong, sweet, and heady. *Leaves* Plentiful, rough-textured. Deep green. *Blooming period* Midsummer, repeating sporadically until autumn.
• TIPS Best with hard pruning.
• PARENTAGE Unknown.
• ORIGIN Uncertain, probably Iran, possibly France, introduced in the 1940s, by Nancy Lindsay.
• OTHER NAMES 'Rose de Rescht', 'Gul e Rescht'.

☀ ◐

Z 4–9

HEIGHT
5ft (1.5m)

SPREAD
4ft (1.2m)

☀ ◐

Z 4–9

HEIGHT
3ft (90cm)

SPREAD
2½ft (75cm)

Sweet briar	

ROSA 'Lady Penzance'

Habit Vigorous, well-branched. *Flowers* Single, slightly cupped, 1½in (4cm) across. Coppery-salmon and pink, with golden stamens. *Scent* Little. *Fruits* Rounded, red hips. *Leaves* Neatly toothed, strongly apple-scented. Mid-green. *Blooming period* Midsummer.
• TIPS Tolerates shade and poorer soils, and suitable for a woodland garden and hedging.
• PARENTAGE *R.eglanteria* x *R. foetida* or *R. foetida* 'Bicolor'.
• ORIGIN Penzance, England, 1894.

☼ ◊

Z 5–8

HEIGHT
6ft (1.8m)
or more

SPREAD
6ft (1.8m)

Species / Wild rose	JAPANESE ROSE, HEDGEHOG ROSE

ROSA RUGOSA

Habit Vigorous, dense, upright. *Flowers* Single, cupped, 3½in (9cm) across. White, or pink-purple. *Scent* Delicate and sweet. *Fruits* Large, round, red hips, often accompanying the later blooms. *Leaves* Leathery, deeply veined, and wrinkled. Dark green, colors well in autumn. *Blooming period* In succession from summer to autumn.
• TIPS Excellent for hedging, especially in coastal gardens, and ideal for massed plantings.
• ORIGIN Coastal areas of E. Russia, Korea, Japan, N. China.

☼ ◊

Z 3–9

HEIGHT
4–8ft
(1.2–2.5m)

SPREAD
4–8ft
(1.2–2.5m)

Species / Wild rose hybrid	

ROSA MOYESII 'Geranium'

Habit Vigorous, upright, arching. *Flowers* Single, cupped to flat, 2in (5cm) across, along the stems. Dusky crimson-scarlet, with creamy-gold stamens. *Scent* Little. *Fruits* Profuse, scarlet hips. *Leaves* Small. Bluish-green. *Blooming period* Summer.
• TIPS Excellent as a specimen; better suited to smaller gardens than the species. Attracts bees. Large hips attractive in autumn. Prune lightly after flowering, and cut out old wood at the base.
• ORIGIN RHS, England, 1938.
• OTHER NAMES *R. moyesii* 'Geranium'.

☼ ◊

Z 4–9

HEIGHT
8ft (2.5m)

SPREAD
5ft (1.5m)

Bourbon	

ROSA 'Mme. Isaac Pereire'

Habit Vigorous, open, arching. *Flowers* Fully double, cupped to quartered-rosette, 6in (15cm) across. Deep cerise-purple; early flowers may be malformed, but later blooms usually perfect. *Scent* Excellent, rich, pervasive, reminiscent of raspberries. *Leaves* Matte. Mid-green. *Blooming period* Repeating from summer to autumn.
• TIPS Best with support of open trellis. Rather susceptible to mildew.
• PARENTAGE Unknown.
• ORIGIN Garçon, France, 1881.

☼ ◊

Z 5–9

HEIGHT
7ft (2.2m)

SPREAD
6ft (2m)

Moss	

ROSA 'Henri Martin'

Habit Vigorous, upright, arching with the weight of bloom. *Flowers* Fully double, rounded, 3in (8cm) across. Rich crimson, revealing golden stamens when fully open; has sparse, light green mossing. *Scent* Strong and sweet. *Leaves* Plentiful. Fresh green. *Blooming period* Midsummer.

• TIPS A very cold-hardy rose that is tolerant of hot, dry summers and light shade. It can be used in north-facing situations. It is very floriferous, bearing its wiry-stemmed flowers along the length of flexible canes. It is best displayed when trained on a tripod, pyramidal trellis, or other strong support, so that the flowering stems can cascade gracefully down almost to ground level. Prune lightly immediately after flowering.

• PARENTAGE Unknown.
• ORIGIN Laffay, France, 1863.
• OTHER NAMES 'Red Moss'.

☼ ◊

Z 4–9

HEIGHT
6ft (1.8m)

SPREAD
4ft (1.2m)

Gallica	

ROSA 'Belle de Crécy'

Habit Rather lax, usually smooth-stemmed.
Flowers Fully double, quartered-rosette, 3in (8cm) across, opening flat to reveal a green button eye. Petals are deep cerise-pink with mauve tones, fading to soft pale violet and lavender-gray. **Scent** Sweet, spicy, intense. **Leaves** Matte. Gray-green. **Blooming period** Midsummer.
• TIPS At its best in fertile soil and a warm, sunny site sheltered from strong winds.
• PARENTAGE Unknown.
• ORIGIN Perhaps introduced by Roeser before 1829.

☼ ◊

Z 4–9

HEIGHT
4ft (1.2m)

SPREAD
3ft (1m)

Gallica	

ROSA 'Cardinal de Richelieu'

Habit Lax, bushy, smooth-stemmed. **Flowers** Fully double, rounded, 3in (8cm) across. Deep mauve, fading to rich burgundy, the velvety petals reflexing, sometimes to reveal a green button eye. **Scent** Moderately strong. **Leaves** Smooth. Dark green. **Blooming period** Midsummer.
• TIPS Good for hedging and mixed borders. Provide fertile soil, prune moderately hard, and remove old, unproductive stems after flowering.
• PARENTAGE Unknown.
• ORIGIN Laffay, France, 1840.

☼ ◊

Z 4–9

HEIGHT
3ft (90cm)

SPREAD
4ft (1.2m)

Moss	

ROSA 'William Lobb'

Habit Vigorous, upright, arching. **Flowers** Double, rosette, 3½in (9cm) across, often in large clusters on bowed stems. Deep crimson-purple, fading, with dove-gray, cerise, and mauve tones. Has dark, heavy mossing. **Scent** Sweet. **Leaves** Large, plentiful. Dark green. **Blooming period** Midsummer.
• TIPS Good for pillars, tripods, or pergolas.
• PARENTAGE Unknown.
• ORIGIN Laffay, France, 1855.
• OTHER NAMES 'Duchesse d'Istrie', 'Old Velvet Moss'.

☼ ◊

Z 4–9

HEIGHT
6ft (1.8m)

SPREAD
6ft (1.8m)

Hybrid Perpetual	

ROSA 'Reine des Violettes'

Habit Vigorous, spreading, with few thorns. **Flowers** Fully double, quartered-rosette, opening flat, 3in (8cm) across. Deep red-violet, with shades of violet and gray as they age. **Scent** Heady and rich. **Leaves** Plentiful, glossy. Gray-green. **Blooming period** Repeating profusely from summer to autumn.
• TIPS Flowers profusely in well-mulched, moist, well-drained soil. May be grown on a support.
• PARENTAGE Seedling of 'Pius IX'.
• ORIGIN Millet-Malet, France, 1860.
• OTHER NAMES 'Queen of the Violets'.

☼ ◊

Z 5–9

HEIGHT
to 6ft (2m)

SPREAD
to 6ft (2m)

Gallica | Hybrid Perpetual

ROSA 'Tuscany Superb'

Habit Vigorous, upright. **Flowers** Double, cupped, 2in (5cm) across, opening flat, with velvety deep crimson petals, aging to purple, with golden stamens. **Scent** Sweet. **Leaves** Plentiful. Dark green. **Blooming period** Midsummer.
• TIPS Good for a group, hedging, or for large containers. Tolerates poorer soils, but best in an open site. Prune away old, unproductive stems.
• PARENTAGE Seedling of 'Tuscany'.
• ORIGIN Rivers, England, 1837.
• OTHER NAMES 'Double Velvet', 'Double Tuscany'.

☼ ◐

Z 4–9

HEIGHT
3½ft (1.1m)

SPREAD
3ft (1m)

ROSA 'Empereur du Maroc'

Habit Upright. **Flowers** Fully double, rather muddled, quartered-rosette, 3in (8cm) across, borne in large heavy clusters. Dark maroon-crimson. **Scent** Intense, sweet. **Leaves** Glossy, dark green. **Blooming period** Midsummer, with later, lesser flushes.
• TIPS Prone to blackspot and mildew. Needs good, fertile soil and shade from the hottest summer sun. Best with support; the heavy flowers weigh down the stems.
• PARENTAGE Seedling of 'Géant de Batailles'.
• ORIGIN Guinoisseau–Flon, France, 1858.

☼ ◐

Z 5–9

HEIGHT
4ft (1.2m)

SPREAD
3ft (1m)

Centifolia | Moss

ROSA 'Tour de Malakoff'

Habit Open, lax, arching. **Flowers** Fully double, rosette, 5in (12cm) across. Magenta-purple, veined violet, fading to grayish-violet. **Scent** Sweet, rich, and heady. **Leaves** Plentiful. Mid-green. **Blooming period** Midsummer.
• TIPS Benefits from some support. Cut back flowered stems by half after flowering.
• PARENTAGE Uncertain, possibly a Bourbon x Gallica.
• ORIGIN Soupert and Notting, Luxembourg, 1856.
• OTHER NAMES 'Black Jack'.

☼ ◐

Z 4–9

HEIGHT
6ft (2m)

SPREAD
5ft (1.5m)

ROSA 'Nuits de Young'

Habit Upright, open, wiry-stemmed. **Flowers** Double, flat, 2in (5cm) across. Deep maroon-purple, with velvety petals and dark red-brown mossing. **Scent** Delicate and fruity. **Leaves** Small. Dark green. **Blooming period** Midsummer.
• TIPS Provides excellent, rich, dark contrast for lighter colors in a mixed border. Needs moist, well-drained fertile soil. Prune after flowering.
• PARENTAGE Unknown.
• ORIGIN Laffay, France, 1845.
• OTHER NAMES 'Old Black'.

☼ ◐

Z 4–9

HEIGHT
4ft (1.2m)

SPREAD
3ft (1m)

Species / Wild rose	INCENSE ROSE, TIEN SHAN ROSE

ROSA PRIMULA

Habit Lax, arching. *Flowers* Single, cupped, 1½in (4cm) across, borne singly along slender, arching branches. Primrose-yellow, fading to pale creamy-yellow. *Scent* Light and delicate. *Fruits* Small, almost spherical, maroon. *Leaves* Plentiful, very aromatic after rain, fern-like. Mid-green, red-brown when young. *Blooming period* Late spring.

• TIPS Related to *R. hugonis*, it bears its delicate flowers along the length of branches clothed with elegantly divided foliage. It is ideal for a ,

sheltered position, such as a courtyard or walled garden, where still air can trap the scent of its foliage.

• ORIGIN Introduced by Meyer from Samarkand, C. Asia, 1910.

• OTHER NAMES *R. ecae* subsp. *primula*.

☼ ◊

Z 5–9

HEIGHT
6ft (2m)

SPREAD
6ft (2m)

Species / Wild rose	AUSTRIAN BRIAR, AUSTRIAN YELLOW

ROSA FOETIDA

Habit Upright, arching, open. **Flowers** Single, cupped, 2in (5cm) across, singly or in pairs, on chocolate stems. Bright yellow, with prominent stamens. **Scent** Distinctly un-roselike. **Fruits** Rounded, dark brick-red. **Leaves** Aromatic, matte. Pale green. **Blooming period** Early summer.
• TIPS Good for a shrub or mixed border. Best in a warm, sheltered site; may die back in hard winters. Susceptible to blackspot.
• ORIGIN S.W. Asia, in scrub and on rocky hillsides.
• OTHER NAMES R. lutea.

☼ ◊

Z 5–8

HEIGHT
5ft (1.5m)

SPREAD
5ft (1.5m)

Species / Wild rose	

ROSA ECAE

Habit Upright, wiry, well-branched, suckering. **Flowers** Single, cupped, ¾in (2cm) across, borne all along red stems. Bright yellow. **Scent** Sweet and musky. **Fruits** Small, round, shiny, red-brown. **Leaves** Small, aromatic, fern-like. Grayish-green. **Blooming period** Early summer.
• TIPS Needs a warm sheltered site in well-drained soil.
• ORIGIN Rocky hillsides, Afghanistan. Introduced in 1880.
• OTHER NAMES R. xanthina var. ecae.

☼ ◊

Z 5–8

HEIGHT
5ft (1.5m)

SPREAD
4ft (1.2m)

Species / Wild rose hybrid	

ROSA XANTHINA 'Canary Bird'

Habit Vigorous, dense, arching. **Flowers** Single, cupped, 2in (5cm) across, along the stems. Clear yellow, with golden stamens. **Scent** Musky. **Fruits** Round, red-black. **Leaves** Small, ferny. Mid-green. **Blooming period** Late spring, may repeat in autumn.
• TIPS Excellent as a specimen plant, and good for hedging. Best in fertile soil in an open site.
• PARENTAGE Possibly R. hugonis × R. xanthina or a seedling of R. xanthina f. spontanea.
• ORIGIN Uncertain, after 1907.
• OTHER NAMES 'Canary Bird'.

☼ ◊

Z 5–8

HEIGHT
to 10ft (3m)

SPREAD
12ft (4m)

Ground cover	

ROSA 'Kent'

Habit Dense, rounded. ***Flowers*** Semi-double, slightly cupped, 2in (5cm) across, opening from neat, pointed buds, in clusters. Creamy-white, lemon tinted at base. ***Scent*** Little. ***Leaves*** Plentiful. Rich, glossy green. ***Blooming period*** Summer to autumn.
• TIPS Suitable for ground cover, bedding, borders, and containers. May be grown as a standard.
• PARENTAGE Not disclosed
• ORIGIN Poulsen, Denmark, 1988.
• OTHER NAMES 'Poulcov', 'Pyrenees', 'White Cover', 'Sparkler'.

☼ ◊

Z 5–9

HEIGHT
22in (55cm)

SPREAD
3ft (1m)

Ground cover	

ROSA 'Blenheim'

Habit Bushy, rounded, spreading, vigorous. ***Flowers*** Double, flat, 2½in (5cm) across, in many-flowered clusters. Blush-white, opening from scrolled, creamy buds. ***Scent*** Fairly strong, sweet, and fresh. ***Leaves*** Plentiful, glossy. Dark green. ***Blooming period*** Continuously from summer to autumn.
• TIPS Excellent ground cover, good for bedding and borders, and suitable for cutting.
• PARENTAGE Not disclosed
• ORIGIN Tantau, Germany, 1990.
• OTHER NAMES 'Tanmurse', 'Schneesturm'.

☼ ◊

Z 5–9

HEIGHT
3ft (1m)

SPREAD
4½ft (1.4m)

Ground cover	

ROSA 'Swany'

Habit Dense, low-spreading. ***Flowers*** Fully double, cupped, 2in (5cm) across, opening flat, borne in showy sprays. White. ***Scent*** Little. ***Leaves*** Plentiful, glossy. Dark green. ***Blooming period*** Summer to autumn.
• TIPS Very hardy and reliable. Excellent for ground cover, or when cascading over a wall, bank, or terrace. May also be grown as a standard.
• PARENTAGE *R. sempervirens* x 'Mlle. Marthe Carron'
• ORIGIN Meilland, France, 1978.
• OTHER NAMES 'Meiburenac'.

☼ ◊

Z 5–9

HEIGHT
to 30in
(75cm)

SPREAD
6ft (2m)

Ground cover	

ROSA 'Northamptonshire'

Habit Vigorous, rather open, dainty, spreading. ***Flowers*** Semi-double, cupped, 1½–2in (4–5cm) across, borne in large, many-flowered clusters. Pearl-pink. ***Scent*** Light and sweet. ***Leaves*** Abundant. ***Blooming period*** Summer to autumn.
• TIPS Good ground cover for a sunny bank, th front of a border, or to cascade over a terrace.
• PARENTAGE Not disclosed.
• ORIGIN Mattock, England, 1988.
• OTHER NAMES 'Mattdor'.

☼ ◊

Z 5–9

HEIGHT
18in (45cm)

SPREAD
3ft (90cm)

Ground cover

ROSA 'Nozomi'

Habit Creeping, stem-rooting, mound-forming, or low-climbing. **Flowers** Single, flat, 1in (2.5cm) across, in delicate clusters, just above the foliage. Pale blush-pink to white, **Scent** Little. **Leaves** Plentiful, small, narrow, shiny dark green, red-tinted. **Blooming period** Midsummer.
• TIPS Excellent ground cover, especially in a rock garden. Prune old stems in winter to keep it low.
• PARENTAGE 'Fairy Princess' x 'Sweet Fairy'.
• ORIGIN Onodera, Japan, 1968.
• OTHER NAMES 'Heideröslein'

☀: ◊

Z 5–9

HEIGHT
18in (45cm)
or more

SPREAD
5ft (1.5m)

Ground cover

ROSA 'Surrey'

Habit Dense, mound-forming, spreading. **Flowers** Double, cupped, 2½in (6cm) across, in clusters along stems. Salmon-pink, with heart-shaped petals. **Scent** Fresh and sweet. **Leaves** Plentiful, glossy. Dark green. **Blooming period** From summer to autumn.
• TIPS Good ground cover on a sunny bank. Also suitable for a border, low hedge, or as a standard.
• PARENTAGE 'The Fairy' x unknown seedling.
• ORIGIN Kordes, Germany, 1985
• OTHER NAMES 'Korlanum', 'Sommerwind', 'Vent d'Été'.

☀: ◊

Z 5–9

HEIGHT
32in (80cm)

SPREAD
4ft (1.2m)

Ground cover

ROSA 'Grouse'

Habit Vigorous, creeping, mound-forming. **Flowers** Single, flat, 1½in (4cm) across, just above the leaves. Pale blush-pink, with golden stamens. **Scent** Sweet fragrance. **Leaves** Small, abundant. Glossy green. **Blooming period** Mid- to late summer; not repeating.
• TIPS Good ground cover for a border front, sunny bank, terrace. Also as a weeping standard. Prune when dormant to reduce height.
• PARENTAGE 'The Fairy' x R. wichuraiana.
• ORIGIN Kordes, Germany, 1984.
• OTHER NAMES 'Korimro', 'Immensee', 'Lac Rose'.

☀: ◊

Z 5–9

HEIGHT
2–4ft
(60–120cm)

SPREAD
to 10ft (3m)

Ground cover

ROSA 'Pink Bells'

Habit Very dense, spreading. **Flowers** Fully double, rosette, 1½in (4cm) across, borne in clusters along the length of the stems. Clear rose-pink. **Scent** Little. **Leaves** Small, plentiful. Dark green. **Blooming period** In midsummer.
• TIPS Excellent dense ground cover for the front of a border or sunny bank. May also be trained over a low fence.
• PARENTAGE 'Mini-Poul' x 'Temple Bells'.
• ORIGIN Poulsen, Denmark, 1983.
• OTHER NAMES 'Poulbells'

☀: ◊

Z 5–9

HEIGHT
2½ft (75cm)

SPREAD
5ft (1.5m)

Ground cover	

ROSA 'Hertfordshire'

Habit Compact, spreading, uneven. *Flowers* Single, cupped to flat, 2in (5cm) across, borne in many-flowered clusters just above the foliage. Carmine-pink, paler at the base, *Scent* Light and pleasant. *Leaves* Plentiful, small, glossy. Rich green. *Blooming period* From summer to autumn, with good continuity.

• TIPS Excellent ground cover for a border front, sunny bank, terrace, or to cascade over the edge of a large container. An easily grown rose that is particularly valuable for its long season of color and interest. It needs little pruning. As with other ground-cover roses, it is essential to clear the ground of all perennial weeds before planting.

• PARENTAGE Not disclosed.

• ORIGIN Kordes, Germany, 1991.

• OTHER NAMES 'Kortenay', 'Tommeliese'.

☼ ◊

Z 5–9

HEIGHT
18in (45cm)

SPREAD
3ft (90cm)

Ground cover

ROSA 'Wiltshire'

Habit Dense, compact, spreading. **Flowers** Double, rounded, 2½in (6cm) across, in large, showy clusters. Deep reddish-pink. **Scent** Light and pleasant. **Leaves** Plentiful, glossy. Mid-green. **Blooming period** Summer to autumn.
- TIPS Good for containers and as ground cover at the front of a border, on a sunny bank, or for cascading over a wall.
- PARENTAGE 'Partridge' × seedling.
- ORIGIN Kordes, Germany, 1993.
- OTHER NAMES 'Kormuse'.

☼ ◊

Z 5–9

HEIGHT 2ft (60cm)

SPREAD 4ft (1.2m)

Ground cover

ROSA 'Berkshire'

Habit Dense, spreading. **Flowers** Semi-double, cupped, 2in (5cm) across, freely borne in neatly spaced clusters. Cherry-pink, with a central boss of golden stamens. **Scent** Delicate and sweet. **Leaves** Plentiful, glossy. Dark bluish-green. **Blooming period** From summer to autumn.
- TIPS Excellent ground cover for a sunny bank or containers. Prune lightly when dormant.
- PARENTAGE 'Partridge' × seedling.
- ORIGIN Kordes, Germany, 1991.
- OTHER NAMES 'Korpinka', 'Pink Sunsation'.

☼ ◊

Z 5–9

HEIGHT 20in (50cm)

SPREAD 4ft (1.2m)

Ground cover

ROSA 'Suma'

Habit Dense, creeping and mound-forming, or low-climbing. **Flowers** Fully double, rosette, 1in (2.5cm) across, in clusters along stems. Ruby-red to deep pink, often white-rimmed. **Scent** Little. **Leaves** Small, abundant, glossy. Dark green, turning crimson in autumn. **Blooming period** Summer to autumn.
- TIPS Good ground cover, for containers, or as a weeping standard. Climbs with support.
- PARENTAGE Seedling of 'Nozomi'.
- ORIGIN Onodera, Japan, 1989.
- OTHER NAMES 'Harsuma'.

☼ ◊

Z 5–9

HEIGHT 2ft (60cm)

SPREAD 5ft (1.5m)

Ground cover

ROSA 'Chilterns'

Habit Vigorous, spreading. **Flowers** Semi-double, cupped, 1–2in (2.5–5cm) across, borne in many-flowered clusters. Deep crimson with yellow stamens. **Scent** Little. **Leaves** Small, glossy. Dark green. **Blooming period** Summer to late autumn.
- TIPS Good ground cover for a sunny bank, border front, or terrace.
- PARENTAGE Not disclosed.
- ORIGIN Kordes, Germany, 1990.
- OTHER NAMES 'Kortemma', 'Fiery Sunsation', 'Mainaufeuer'.

☼ ◊

Z 5–9

HEIGHT 2½ft (75cm)

SPREAD 7ft (2.2m)

Ground cover	

ROSA 'Red Meidiland'

Habit Very dense, spreading. *Flowers* Single, flat, 2in (5cm) across, opening from neatly pointed buds, and borne in showy clusters. Deep bright red with a white eye and a prominent boss of golden stamens. *Scent* Little. *Fruits* Small, orange-red. *Leaves* Small, plentiful, glossy. Light green. *Blooming period* Summer to autumn.
• TIPS A hardy and healthy rose with a very dense habit and abundant foliage that forms excellent ground cover on a sunny bank or terrace wall. It needs little pruning, and produces flowers in profusion over long periods. Its value for color in the garden continues into late autumn with the additional interest of its small, but plentiful, hips.
• PARENTAGE ' Sea Foam' x ('Picasso' x 'Eye Paint').
• ORIGIN Meilland, France, 1989.
• OTHER NAMES 'Meineble', 'Rouge Meillandécar'.

☼ ◊

Z 5–9

HEIGHT
2½ft (75cm)

SPREAD
5ft (1.5m)

Rugosa hybrid	

ROSA × JACKSONII 'Max Graf'

Habit Vigorous, stem-rooting, dense, arching. **Flowers** Single, slightly cupped to flat, 3in (8cm) across, borne close to stems. Pink, paler at the center. **Scent** Sweet, fresh, of apples. **Leaves** Plentiful, glossy. Bright rich green. **Blooming period** Summer.
• TIPS Excellent, weed-smothering ground cover for informal borders or sunny banks. Site in a sunny, open position where it has room to spread.
• PARENTAGE *R. rugosa* x *R. wichuraiana*.
• ORIGIN Bowditch, US, 1919.

☼ ◊
Z 5–9
HEIGHT 2ft (60cm)
SPREAD 8ft (2.5m)

Ground cover	

ROSA 'Broadlands'

Habit Dense, spreading, vigorous. **Flowers** Double, cupped, 3½in (9cm) across, produced in profusion. Pale creamy-yellow, with slightly incurved petals and golden stamens. **Scent** Sweet and fresh. **Leaves** Plentiful, healthy. Mid-green. **Blooming period** From summer to autumn with good continuity.
• TIPS Excellent ground cover for sunny banks and borders. Suitable for large containers.
• PARENTAGE Not disclosed.
• ORIGIN Tantau, Germany, 1993.
• OTHER NAMES 'Tanmirsch', 'Sonnenschirm'.

☼ ◊
Z 5–9
HEIGHT 2½ft (75cm)
SPREAD 4½ft (1.3m)

Ground cover	

ROSA 'Flower Carpet'

Habit Dense, spreading, vigorous. **Flowers** Double, cupped, 2in (5cm) across, borne in showy, many-flowered clusters. Deep rose-pink. **Scent** Little. **Leaves** Plentiful, glossy. Rich green. **Blooming period** Summer to autumn or early winter.
• TIPS Useful ground cover for a sunny bank, border, or terrace. May be grown in large containers or as a standard.
• PARENTAGE 'Grouse' x 'Amanda'.
• ORIGIN Noack, Germany, 1991.
• OTHER NAMES 'Heidetraum', 'Noatraum'.

☼ ◊
Z 5–9
HEIGHT 2½ft (75cm)
SPREAD 4ft (1.2m)

Ground cover	

ROSA 'Norfolk'

Habit Dense, bushy, neat. **Flowers** Double, rosette, 2in (5cm) across, borne in many-flowered clusters. Bright yellow. **Scent** Light and delicate. **Leaves** Plentiful, rather small, glossy. Mid-green. **Blooming period** From summer to autumn.
• TIPS Suitable for limited ground cover. Useful where space is at a premium. May also be grown in large containers.
• PARENTAGE Not disclosed.
• ORIGIN Poulsen, Denmark, 1990.
• OTHER NAMES 'Poulfolk'.

☼ ◊
Z 5–9
HEIGHT 18in (45cm)
SPREAD 24in (60cm)

Dwarf Sempervirens	

ROSA 'White Pet'

Habit Bushy, mound-forming. **Flowers** Fully double, pompon, 1½in (4cm) across, in large, many-flowered clusters, in profusion. White, pink in bud. **Scent** Sweet and delicate. **Leaves** Plentiful, small. Bluish-green. **Blooming period** Summer to autumn.
• TIPS Tolerates partial shade, but best in an open site in fertile soil. Excellent for the front of a border, for containers, or as a standard.
• PARENTAGE Sport/seedling of 'Félicité Perpétue'.
• ORIGIN Henderson, US, 1879.
• OTHER NAMES 'Little White Pet'.

☼ ◊

Z 5–9

HEIGHT
18in (45cm)

SPREAD
22in (55cm)

Ground cover	

ROSA 'Avon'

Habit Dense, creeping, low-spreading. **Flowers** Semi-double, cupped, 1½in (4cm) across, in many-flowered clusters. Blush- to pearly-white, with golden stamens. **Scent** Little. **Leaves** Plentiful, glossy. Mid-green. **Blooming period** Summer to autumn.
• TIPS Excellent for containers, window boxes, and for group plantings at the front of a border or in a raised bed.
• PARENTAGE 'Pink Drift' x seedling
• ORIGIN Poulsen, Denmark, 1992.
• OTHER NAMES 'Poulmulti'.

☼ ◊

Z 5–9

HEIGHT
12in (30cm)

SPREAD
3ft (90cm)

Polyantha	

ROSA 'Yvonne Rabier'

Habit Bushy, dense, compact. **Flowers** Double, rounded, 2in (5cm) across, in abundant clusters. Creamy-white. **Scent** Sweet, fresh, and delicate. **Leaves** Plentiful, small, slender, glossy. Bright green. **Blooming period** Through summer and autumn.
• TIPS Excellent for massed plantings or for the front of a border. Grows best in fertile, humus-rich, moist but well-drained soil, in an open site.
• PARENTAGE R. wichuraiana x a Polyantha.
• ORIGIN Turbat, France, 1910.

☼ ◊

Z 5–9

HEIGHT
18–28in
(45–70cm)

SPREAD
16in (40cm)

Miniature bush	

ROSA 'Snowball'

Habit Compact, slightly spreading. **Flowers** Fully double, pompon, 1in (2.5cm) across, with many narrow petals, borne in clusters. Creamy-white. **Scent** Little. **Leaves** Plentiful, with tiny, bright green leaflets. **Blooming period** Summer to autumn.
• TIPS Excellent for containers, including window boxes and confined spaces. Prefers fertile soil and an open site.
• PARENTAGE 'Moana' x 'Snow Carpet'
• ORIGIN McGredy, New Zealand, 1984.
• OTHER NAMES 'Macangel', 'Angelita'.

☼ ◊

Z 5–9

HEIGHT
8in (20cm)

SPREAD
12in (30cm)

Miniature ground cover

ROSA 'Snow Carpet'

Habit Prostrate, creeping. **Flowers** Fully double, pompon, 1¼in (3cm) across, borne in sprays just above the foliage. Creamy-white with pointed petals. **Scent** Little. **Leaves** Small, narrow, plentiful, glossy. Clear bright green. **Blooming period** Midsummer, sometimes producing a few flowers in autumn.

• TIPS A rose of creeping habit, eventually forming a low mound of abundant, glossy foliage that is studded in midsummer with delicate, almost starry flowers. Provides excellent ground cover on a sunny bank, at the front of a border, or in a rock garden. Repeat blooming is often more profuse following a long, hot summer. Also attractive as a miniature standard.

• PARENTAGE 'New Penny' x 'Temple Bells'.
• ORIGIN McGredy, New Zealand, 1980.
• OTHER NAMES 'Maccarpe'.

☼ ◊

Z 5–9

HEIGHT
6in (15cm)

SPREAD
20in (50cm)

Dwarf cluster-flowered shrub (Patio shrub)	

ROSA 'Pretty Polly'

Habit Neat, dense, rounded. **Flowers** Double, urn-shaped, cupped when open, 2in (5cm) across, in many-flowered clusters. Clear rose-pink. **Scent** Light. **Leaves** Small, plentiful, glossy. Mid-green. **Blooming period** Freely from summer to autumn.
• TIPS Excellent for containers, bedding, the front of a border, and as a standard.
• PARENTAGE 'Coppélia '76' × 'Magic Carrousel'.
• ORIGIN Meilland, France, 1989.
• OTHER NAMES 'Meitonje', 'Pink Symphony', 'Sweet Sunblaze'.

☼ ◐

Z 5–9

HEIGHT
16in (40cm)

SPREAD
18in (45cm)

Dwarf cluster-flowered bush (Patio bush)	

ROSA 'Gentle Touch'

Habit Dense, bushy, upright. **Flowers** Double, semi-cupped, 2in (5cm) across, opening from urn-shaped buds, in well-filled clusters. Pale pink. **Scent** Light and sweet. **Leaves** Plentiful, small, glossy. Dark green. **Blooming period** Summer to autumn.
• TIPS Excellent for cutting, ground cover, low hedging, containers, or as a standard.
• PARENTAGE 'Liverpool Echo' × ('Woman's Own' × 'Memento').
• ORIGIN Dickson, Northern Ireland, 1986.
• OTHER NAMES 'Diclulu'.

☼ ◐

Z 5–9

HEIGHT
16in (40cm)

SPREAD
16in (40cm)

Dwarf cluster flowered shrub (Patio shrub)	

ROSA 'Queen Mother'

Habit Dense, spreading. **Flowers** Semi-double, almost flat, 2½–3in (6–8cm) across, from pointed buds, in many-flowered clusters. Clear pink. **Scent** Light. **Leaves** Plentiful, small, glossy. Dark green. **Blooming period** Freely from summer to autumn.
• TIPS Excellent for a sunny bank, border front, container, or as a standard. Prune lightly.
• PARENTAGE R. wichuraiana seedling × 'Toynbee Hall'.
• ORIGIN Kordes, Germany, 1991.
• OTHER NAMES 'Korquemu'.

☼ ◐

Z 5–9

HEIGHT
18in (45cm)

SPREAD
24in (60cm)

Ground cover	

ROSA 'Harewood'

Habit Dense, spreading. **Flowers** Semi-double, cupped, 2in (5cm) across, in clusters. Dusky pink, fading paler pink with a creamy-white center. **Scent** Light and sweet. **Leaves** Small, plentiful, glossy. Mid-green. **Blooming period** Summer to autumn.
• TIPS Excellent for ground cover on a sunny bank or for a border front. Prune away dead or weak wood to keep the plant healthy.
• PARENTAGE Not disclosed.
• ORIGIN Tantau, Germany, 1995.
• OTHER NAMES 'Taninaso'.

☼ ◐

Z 5–9

HEIGHT
2ft (60cm)

SPREAD
3½ft (1.1m)

Ground cover	

Rosa 'Chatsworth'

Habit Dense, spreading, with arching stems.
Flowers Double, cupped, 2½in (6cm) across,
borne in many-flowered clusters. Rich, deep pink.
Scent Sweet and fresh. *Leaves* Small, plentiful,
glossy. Dark green. *Blooming period* From
summer to autumn.
• TIPS Excellent for containers or as ground cover.
May also be grown as a standard.
• PARENTAGE Not disclosed
• ORIGIN Tantau, Germany, 1990.
• OTHER NAMES 'Tanotax', 'Mirato', 'Tanotari'.

☼ ◊

Z 5–9

HEIGHT
2ft (60cm)

SPREAD
to 3½ft
(1.1m)

Miniature bush	

Rosa 'Angela Rippon'

Habit Bushy. *Flowers* Fully double, urn-shaped,
1½in (4cm) across, opening flat. Salmon-pink.
Scent Light and delicate. *Leaves* Plentiful, small.
Dark green. *Blooming period* Summer to autumn.
• TIPS Excellent for containers, window boxes, and
for group plantings at the front of a border or in a
raised bed. The small blooms are good for
miniature arrangements and exhibition.
• PARENTAGE 'Rosy Jewel' × 'Zorina'
• ORIGIN De Ruiter, The Netherlands, 1978.
• OTHER NAMES 'Ocarina', 'Ocaru'.

☼ ◊

Z 5–9

HEIGHT
18in (45cm)

SPREAD
12in (30cm)

Miniature bush	

Rosa 'Stacey Sue'

Habit Bushy, upright, slightly spreading. *Flowers*
Fully double, rosette, 1in (2.5cm) across, borne in
large, well-spaced clusters. Medium pink. *Scent*
Little. *Leaves* Plentiful, small, narrow, pointed,
glossy. Dark green. *Blooming period* From
summer to autumn.
• TIPS Excellent for smaller containers,
including window boxes, confined spaces, and
exhibition.
• PARENTAGE 'Ellen Poulsen' × 'Fairy Princess'.
• ORIGIN Moore, US, 1976.

☼ ◊

Z 5–9

HEIGHT
10in (25cm)

SPREAD
12in (30cm)

Miniature bush	

ROSA 'Hula Girl'

Habit Upright, bushy, neat. *Flowers* Fully double, urn-shaped, 1in (2.5cm) across, with pointed petals, borne in profusion. Pale salmon-orange. *Scent* Fruity. *Leaves* Plentiful, leathery, glossy. Mid-green. *Blooming period* Summer to autumn.
• TIPS Excellent for bedding, borders, and containers; useful for showing. Remove dead wood in winter.
• PARENTAGE 'Miss Hillcrest' x 'Mabel Dot'.
• ORIGIN Williams, US, 1975.

☼ ◊

Z 5–9

HEIGHT
18in (45cm)

SPREAD
16in (40cm)

Miniature bush	

ROSA 'Fire Princess'

Habit Compact, upright, vigorous. *Flowers* Fully double, cupped rosette, 1½in (4cm) across, borne in sprays. Rich scarlet. *Scent* Little. *Leaves* Plentiful, small, leathery, dark green. *Blooming period* Repeats well from summer to autumn.
• TIPS Tolerates a range of climates; best in fertile soil in an open site. Good for bedding, containers, confined spaces, and for showing. Lightly prune away twiggy growth, and shorten vigorous growth.
• PARENTAGE 'Baccará' x 'Eleanor'.
• ORIGIN Moore, US, 1969.

☼ ◊

Z 5–9

HEIGHT
18in (45cm)

SPREAD
12in (30cm)

Dwarf cluster-flowered bush (Patio bush)	

ROSA 'Anna Ford'

Habit Bushy, dense, low-spreading. *Flowers* Semi-double, urn-shaped in bud, opening flat, 1½in (4cm) across, borne in many-flowered clusters. Rich orange-red, with a yellow center. *Scent* Little. *Leaves* Small, glossy. Dark green. *Blooming period* Freely throughout summer and autumn.
• TIPS Excellent for containers, low hedges, and bedding. Cut out dead or weak growth in winter.
• PARENTAGE 'Southampton' x 'Darling Flame'.
• ORIGIN Harkness, England, 1981.
• OTHER NAMES 'Harpiccolo'.

☼ ◊

Z 5–9

HEIGHT
18in (45cm)

SPREAD
15in (38cm)

Dwarf cluster-flowered bush (Patio bush)	

ROSA 'Wee Jock'

Habit Dense, bushy. *Flowers* Fully double, high-centered in bud, opening rosette, 1½in (4cm) across, borne in many-flowered clusters. Deep crimson. *Scent* Light and sweet. *Leaves* Plentiful, small. Dark green. *Blooming period* Freely from summer to autumn.
• TIPS Excellent for cutting, containers, border front, and confined spaces. Prune lightly.
• PARENTAGE 'National Trust' x 'Wee Man'.
• ORIGIN Cocker, Scotland, 1980.
• OTHER NAMES 'Cocabest'.

☼ ◊

Z 5–9

HEIGHT
18in (45cm)

SPREAD
18in (15cm)

Miniature bush	

ROSA 'Sheri Anne'

Habit Upright, compact. **Flowers** Double, rosette, 1in (2.5cm) across, borne in open, many-flowered clusters. Light red. **Scent** Little. **Leaves** Small, plentiful, leathery, glossy. Clear green. **Blooming period** From summer to autumn.
• TIPS Good for cutting and exhibition, this hardy and healthy rose flowers reliably over long periods; the brightly colored flowers eventually open fully to reveal a boss of golden stamens. It grows best in an open, sunny site, and in fertile soil, and needs only light pruning. It is also ideal for containers, and even suitable for a large window box. Apply a balanced liquid fertilizer to container-grown plants at monthly intervals during the growing season.
• PARENTAGE 'Little Darling' × 'New Penny'.
• ORIGIN Moore, US, 1973.
• OTHER NAMES 'Morsheri'.

☼ ◊

Z 5–9

HEIGHT
12in (30cm)

SPREAD
10in (25cm)

Miniature bush

ROSA 'Red Ace'

Habit Dense, compact, upright. **Flowers** Semi-double, rosette, 1½in (4cm) across. Rich, deep crimson. **Scent** Little. **Leaves** Small, plentiful, glossy. Dark green. **Blooming period** From summer to autumn.
• TIPS Excellent for cutting, exhibition, and containers, including window boxes. Prune lightly to keep tidy, and cut out weak growth in winter.
• PARENTAGE 'Scarletta' x seedling.
• ORIGIN De Ruiter, The Netherlands, 1982.
• OTHER NAMES 'Amanda', 'Amruda'.

☼ ◌

Z 5–9

HEIGHT
12in (30cm)

SPREAD
12in (30cm)

Dwarf cluster-flowered
bush (Patio bush)

ROSA 'Festival'

Habit Very compact, mound-forming. **Flowers** Fully double, almost flat, 2in (5cm) across, from urn-shaped buds. Rich, velvety scarlet-crimson with a paler petal reverse and irregular white markings. **Scent** Light. **Leaves** Small, plentiful, glossy. Dark bluish-green. **Blooming period** Summer to autumn.
• TIPS Excellent for confined spaces, low bedding, and containers. May be grown as a standard.
• PARENTAGE 'Regensberg' x seedling
• ORIGIN Kordes, Germany, 1994.
• OTHER NAMES 'Kordialo'.

☼ ◌

Z 5–9

HEIGHT
24in (60cm)

SPREAD
20in (50cm)

Dwarf cluster-flowered
bush (Patio bush)

ROSA 'Top Marks'

Habit Rounded, bushy, compact. **Flowers** Fully double, rosette, 1½in (4cm) across, borne in dense, many-flowered clusters. Bright orange-vermilion. **Scent** Little. **Leaves** Plentiful, small, glossy, mid-green. **Blooming period** From summer to autumn.
• TIPS Suitable for containers, bedding, and a border front. May be prone to blackspot.
• PARENTAGE [('Anytime' x 'Liverpool Echo') x ('New Penny' x seedling)] x seedling.
• ORIGIN Fryer, England, 1992.
• OTHER NAMES 'Fryministar'.

☼ ◌

Z 5–9

HEIGHT
16in (40cm)

SPREAD
18in (45cm)

Dwarf cluster-flowered
bush (Patio bush)

ROSA 'Fiesta'

Habit Bushy, irregular. **Flowers** Double, cupped, 2in (5cm) across, in many-flowered clusters. Petals are prettily patterned crimson-pink with a paler edge and white base. **Scent** Little. **Leaves** Plentiful, glossy. Dark green. **Blooming period** From summer to autumn.
• TIPS Useful for cutting, containers, low bedding, or the front of a border.
• PARENTAGE Not known.
• ORIGIN McGredy, New Zealand, 1995.
• OTHER NAMES 'Macfirinlin'.

☼ ◌

Z 5–9

HEIGHT
24in (60cm)

SPREAD
16in (40cm)

Miniature bush	

ROSA 'Blue Peter'

Habit Compact, upright. **Flowers** Double, cupped, 2in (5cm) across. Lavender-purple. **Scent** Light and delicate. **Leaves** Plentiful, small, glossy light green. **Blooming period** Summer to autumn.
• TIPS Excellent for confined spaces or containers. Best in an open site, in fertile soil. Remove dead and weak growth in winter; shorten remaining stems to promote dense new growth.
• PARENTAGE 'Little Flirt' x seedling.
• ORIGIN De Ruiter, The Netherlands, 1982.
• OTHER NAMES 'Azulabria', 'Ruiblun', 'Bluenette'.

☀ ◊

Z 5–9

HEIGHT
14in (35cm)

SPREAD
12in (30cm)

Dwarf cluster-flowered bush (Patio bush)	

ROSA 'Hakuun'

Habit Bushy, compact. **Flowers** Semi-double, pointed, 2in (5cm) across, borne in dense, many-flowered clusters that almost obscure the foliage. Buff to creamy-white. **Scent** Light and sweet. **Leaves** Small, glossy. Mid-green. **Blooming period** Very freely from summer to autumn.
• TIPS Hardy and reliable, needing no special treatment to perform well. Excellent for a border front, containers, bedding, and low hedges.
• PARENTAGE Seedling x ('Pinocchio' selfed).
• ORIGIN Poulsen, Denmark, 1962.

☀ ◊

Z 5–9

HEIGHT
16in (40cm)

SPREAD
18in (45cm)

Dwarf cluster-flowered bush (Patio bush)	

ROSA 'Little Bo-Peep'

Habit Very compact, dense, cushion-like. **Flowers** Semi-double, flat, 1½in (4cm) across, borne in very dense, many-flowered clusters. Pale pink. **Scent** Little. **Leaves** Small, plentiful, glossy. Bluish-green. **Blooming period** Very freely from summer to autumn.
• TIPS Excellent for low bedding, ground cover, a border front, containers, or as a standard.
• PARENTAGE 'Caterpillar' x seedling.
• ORIGIN Poulsen, Denmark, 1992.
• OTHER NAMES 'Poullen'.

☀ ◊

Z 5–9

HEIGHT
12in (30cm)

SPREAD
20in (50cm)

Dwarf cluster-flowered bush (Patio bush)	

ROSA 'Rugul'

Habit Neat, compact. **Flowers** Double, cupped to flat, 2in (5cm) across, with narrow petals, borne in clusters. Yellow. **Scent** Little. **Leaves** Small, plentiful, glossy, rich bright green. **Blooming period** From summer to autumn.
• TIPS Excellent for containers, for the front of a border, or for confined spaces. Best in fertile soil and an open site. Prune lightly in autumn or spring.
• PARENTAGE 'Rosy Jewel' x 'Allgold'.
• ORIGIN De Ruiter, Netherlands, 1973.
• OTHER NAMES 'Guletta', 'Tapis Jaune'.

☀ ◊

Z 5–9

HEIGHT
12in (30cm)

SPREAD
16in (40cm)

Miniature bush	

ROSA 'Rise 'n' Shine'

Habit Bushy, upright. **Flowers** Fully double, rosette, 1½in (4cm) across, with pointed petals, profusely, in clusters. Deep yellow. **Scent** Little. **Leaves** Plentiful, small, pointed. Mid-green. **Blooming period** From summer to autumn.
• TIPS Good for exhibition, containers, low hedging, or a border front. Prune lightly in autumn or spring.
• PARENTAGE 'Little Darling' x 'Yellow Magic'
• ORIGIN Moore, US, 1977.
• OTHER NAMES 'Golden Meillandina', 'Golden Sunblaze'

☀ ◊
—————
Z 5–9

HEIGHT
18in (45cm)

SPREAD
16in (40cm)

Dwarf cluster-flowered bush (Patio bush)	

ROSA 'Shine On'

Habit Rounded, dense, compact. **Flowers** Double, rounded, 2in (5cm) across, in many-flowered clusters. Rich golden-apricot blended with pink. **Scent** Light and delicate. **Leaves** Small, plentiful, glossy dark green. **Blooming period** From summer to autumn.
• TIPS Excellent for cutting, containers. low bedding, or the border front. Prune lightly in spring or autumn.
• PARENTAGE 'Sweet Magic' x (seedling x 'Minni Pol').
• ORIGIN Dickson, Northern Ireland, 1994.
• OTHER NAMES 'Dictalent'.

☀ ◊
—————
Z 5–9

HEIGHT
16in (40cm)

SPREAD
16in (40cm)

Dwarf cluster-flowered bush (Patio bush)	

ROSA 'Sweet Dream'

Habit Bushy, upright, stiff. **Flowers** Fully double, deeply cupped, often quartered, 2½in (6cm) across, in showy clusters. Rich peach-apricot. **Scent** Light. **Leaves** Small, plentiful, matte. Dark green. **Blooming period** Freely from summer to autumn.
• TIPS Excellent for cutting, low bedding, containers, a border front, and as a standard.
• PARENTAGE Seedling x [('Anytime' x 'Liverpool Echo') x ('New Penny' x seedling)].
• ORIGIN Fryer, England, 1988.
• OTHER NAMES 'Fryminicot'.

☀ ◊
—————
Z 5–9

HEIGHT
16in (40cm)

SPREAD
14in (35cm)

Miniature bush	

ROSA 'Baby Masquerade'

Habit Dense, upright, bushy. **Flowers** Double, rosette, 1in (2.5cm) across, in many-flowered clusters. Yellow on opening, then pink, finally tinted dark crimson. **Scent** Little. **Leaves** Tiny, plentiful. Dark green. **Blooming period** Summer to autumn.
• TIPS Suitable for bedding, containers, cutting, or as a standard. Easy to grow.
• PARENTAGE 'Peon' x 'Masquerade'.
• ORIGIN Tantau, Germany, 1956.
• OTHER NAMES 'Baby Carnival', 'Tanbakede', 'Tanba'.

Dwarf cluster-flowered bush (Patio bush)	

ROSA 'Mandarin'

Habit Dense, bushy, compact, vigorous. **Flowers** Double, rosette, 1½in (4cm) across, borne in dense, many-flowered clusters. Deep pink with an orange-yellow center. **Scent** Little. **Leaves** Plentiful, small, glossy. Dark green. **Blooming period** From summer to autumn.
• TIPS Excellent for low bedding, a border front, and containers. Prune lightly in autumn or spring.
• PARENTAGE Not disclosed.
• ORIGIN Kordes, Germany, 1987.
• OTHER NAMES 'Korcelin'.

☼ ◐

Z 5–9

HEIGHT
16in (40cm)

SPREAD
16in (40cm)

☼ ◐

Z 5–9

HEIGHT
16in (40cm)

SPREAD
16in (40cm)

Dwarf cluster-flowered bush (Patio bush)	

ROSA 'Gingernut'

Habit Bushy, rounded, upright. **Flowers** Double, cupped, 3in (8cm) across, borne in many-flowered clusters. Rich orange-bronze, flushed with red and pink. **Scent** Light and sweet. **Leaves** Rather sparse, small, glossy. Dark green. **Blooming period** Summer to autumn.
• TIPS Good for bedding, containers, or ground cover. Prune lightly in spring or autumn.
• PARENTAGE ('Sabine' x 'Circus') x 'Darling Flame'.
• ORIGIN Cocker, Scotland, 1989.
• OTHER NAMES 'Coccrazy'.

☼ ◐

Z 5–9

HEIGHT
f6in (40cm)

SPREAD
18in (45cm)

Dwarf cluster-flowered bush (Patio bush)	

ROSA 'Cider Cup'

Habit Compact, bushy, upright. **Flowers** Double, cupped, 1½–2in (4–5cm) across, opening from high-pointed buds, borne in many-flowered clusters. Deep apricot-pink. **Scent** Little. **Leaves** Small, glossy. Dark green. **Blooming period** From summer to autumn.
• TIPS Excellent for containers, bedding, and cutting. May also be grown as a standard.
• PARENTAGE Seedling of 'Memento'.
• ORIGIN Dickson, Northern Ireland, 1988.
• OTHER NAMES 'Dicladida'.

☼ ◊

Z 5–9

HEIGHT
18in (45cm)

SPREAD
12in (30cm)

Dwarf cluster-flowered bush (Patio bush)	

ROSA 'Sweet Magic'

Habit Bushy, slightly spreading. **Flowers** Double, cupped, 1½in (4cm) across, opening from elegant, pointed buds, in open sprays. Golden-orange, flushed with pink. **Scent** Light, sweet, and delicate. **Leaves** Small, plentiful, glossy. Mid-green. **Blooming period** Freely from summer to autumn.
• TIPS Excellent for low hedging, a border front, or containers. Best in an open site.
• PARENTAGE 'Peek a Boo' x 'Bright Smile'.
• ORIGIN Dickson, Northern Ireland, 1987.
• OTHER NAMES 'Dicmagic'.

☼ ◊

Z 5–9

HEIGHT
16in (40cm)

SPREAD
16in (40cm)

Miniature bush	

ROSA 'Colibri '79'

Habit Upright, open. **Flowers** Double, urn-shaped in bud, then cupped, 1½in (4cm) across. Orange-yellow veined with red-pink. **Scent** Little. **Leaves** Plentiful, glossy. Mid-green. **Blooming period** From summer to autumn.
• TIPS Excellent for containers or confined spaces. Best in an open site. Remove dead and weak growth in winter to promote dense new growth.
• PARENTAGE Not disclosed.
• ORIGIN Meilland, France, 1979.
• OTHER NAMES 'Meidanover', Colibri '80.

☼ ◊

Z 5–9

HEIGHT
12in (30cm)

SPREAD
12in (30cm)

Miniature bush	

ROSA 'Orange Sunblaze'

Habit Neat, dense, compact. **Flowers** Fully double, rosette, 1½in (4cm) across. Bright orange-red. **Scent** Light. **Leaves** Plentiful, pointed, small, glossy. Dark green. **Blooming period** Summer to autumn.
• TIPS Excellent for window boxes, containers, and other confined spaces. Prune lightly.
• PARENTAGE 'Parador' x ('Baby Bettina' x 'Duchess of Windsor').
• ORIGIN Meilland, France, 1981.
• OTHER NAMES 'Orange Meillandina', 'Meijikitar', 'Sunblaze'.

☼ ◊

Z 5–9

HEIGHT
12in (30cm)

SPREAD
12in (30cm)

Dwarf cluster-flowered bush (Patio bush)

ROSA 'Conservation'

Habit Bushy, vigorous. **Flowers** Semi-double, cupped, 2½in (6cm) across, with neatly crimped, petals, borne in short-stemmed clusters. Apricot-pink. **Scent** Light and sweet. **Leaves** Small, plentiful, glossy. Mid-green. **Blooming period** Summer to autumn.

• TIPS Excellent for bedding, to form a group or a low hedge, or in containers. Best in an open site. This and other patio roses are ideal for smaller gardens or other sites where space is at a premium. Deadhead frequently, and, to maintain a neat, dense habit, remove a proportion of the oldest stems in winter, and reduce the remainder by up to one-third of their length.

• PARENTAGE [('Sabine' x 'Circus') x 'Maxi'] x 'Darling Flame'.

• ORIGIN Cocker, Scotland, 1988.

• OTHER NAMES 'Cocdimple'.

☼ ◊

Z 5–9

HEIGHT
18in (45cm)

SPREAD
18in (45cm)

Rambler	

ROSA 'Rambling Rector'

Habit Very vigorous, clambering, arching. **Flowers** Semi-double, flat, 1½–2in (4–5cm) across, in profuse clusters. Creamy-white with golden stamens. **Scent** Sweet and fresh. **Fruits** Small, oval, shining hips. Red. **Leaves** Plentiful, semi-glossy. Light to mid-green. **Blooming period** Once in summer.
• TIPS Ideal for hiding an ugly building or for growing through a large tree. Needs ample space.
• PARENTAGE Uncertain, possibly *R. multiflora* x *R. moschata*.
• ORIGIN Unknown, before 1912.

☀: ◊

Z 4–9

HEIGHT
20ft (6m)
or more

SPREAD
20ft (6m)

Climber	

ROSA 'White Cockade'

Habit Slow-growing, bushy, upright. **Flowers** Fully double, rounded, 4in (10cm) across, pure white. Noted for the very attractive, well-formed blooms. **Scent** Light. **Leaves** Plentiful, large, neat, glossy. Dark green.
Blooming period From summer to autumn, with good continuity.
• TIPS Flowers are good for cutting. Excellent for a wall, fence, or pillar. May also be grown as a shrub.
• PARENTAGE 'New Dawn' x 'Circus'.
• ORIGIN Cocker, Scotland, 1969.

☀: ◊

Z 4–9

HEIGHT
6–10ft
(2–3m)

SPREAD
5ft (1.5m)

Rambler	

ROSA 'Sander's White Rambler'

Habit Vigorous, arching and trailing. **Flowers** Fully double, rosette, 2in (5cm) across, in large, drooping clusters. White, from pink-tinted buds. **Scent** Sweet, pervasive. **Leaves** Plentiful, small, glossy. Mid-green. **Blooming period** After midsummer.
• TIPS Excellent for a tall pillar or pergola; may be grown as ground cover on a sunny bank or to clamber over shrubs, or as a weeping standard.
• PARENTAGE Unknown.
• ORIGIN Unknown, sent to Britain from Belgium, introduced by Sander, England, 1912.

☀: ◊

Z 4–9

HEIGHT
12ft (3.6m)

SPREAD
12ft (3.6m)

Climber

ROSA FILIPES 'Kiftsgate'

Habit Extremely vigorous, rapidly growing, with strong, arching stems. **Flowers** Single, cupped, 1½in (4cm) across, in cascading sprays. Creamy-white. **Scent** Sweet and pervasive, often elusive. **Fruits** Small, oval hips. Red. **Leaves** Large, glossy. Fresh green. **Blooming period** Midsummer.
• TIPS Excellent for growing through mature trees or to hide ugly buildings. Suited only to larger gardens.
• PARENTAGE A form of *R. filipes*.
• ORIGIN Introduced by E. Murrell, England, 1954.
• OTHER NAMES 'Kiftsgate'.

☼ ◐

Z 4–9

HEIGHT
30ft (10m)
or more

SPREAD
22ft (7m)

Climber

ROSA MULLIGANII

Habit Vigorous, clambering, with hooked thorns. **Flowers** Single, flat, 1½–2in (4–5cm) across, in big clusters of up to 150 blooms, drooping on slender pedicels. Creamy-white. **Scent** Light, fresh. **Fruits** Small, round. Orange-scarlet. **Leaves** Large, glossy. Dark green. **Blooming period** Midsummer.
• TIPS Ideal for growing through a large tree in a sheltered site, in a woodland garden, or on a pergola.
• ORIGIN Yunnan, from seed collected by Forrest, sent to Wisley, England, 1919.
• OTHER NAMES *R. longicuspis* misapplied.

☼ ◐

Z 5–9

HEIGHT
15ft (5m)
often more

SPREAD
10ft (3m)

Rambler

ROSA 'Albéric Barbier'

Habit Vigorous, with slender, flexible stems. **Flowers** Fully double and semi-double, rosette, 3in (8cm) across, borne in small, but profuse clusters. Creamy-white, opening from yellow buds. **Scent** Sweet, delicate. **Leaves** Semi-evergreen, glossy. Dark green. **Blooming period** Early to midsummer.
• TIPS Excellent for growing through trees and on pergolas. Tolerates north-facing walls, some shade and poorer soils.
• PARENTAGE *R. wichuraiana* x 'Shirley Hibberd'.
• ORIGIN Barbier, France, 1900.

☼ ◐

Z 5–9

HEIGHT
15ft (5m)
or more

SPREAD
12ft (4m)

Climber

ROSA 'Bobbie James'

Habit Extremely vigorous, with long, thick stems. **Flowers** Semi-double, cupped to flat, 2in (5cm) across, in large, drooping clusters. Creamy-pearl-white. **Scent** Sweet, pervasive. **Leaves** Plentiful, glossy. Fresh green. **Blooming period** Summer.
• TIPS Excellent for concealing unsightly buildings or for growing through sturdy old trees. Must have strong support; site only where space permits.
• PARENTAGE Uncertain, probably involving *R. multiflora*.
• ORIGIN Sunningdale Nurseries, England, 1961.

☼ ◐

Z 4–9

HEIGHT
28ft (9m)

SPREAD
20ft (6m)

Climber	

ROSA 'Félicité Perpétue'

Habit Vigorous, arching. *Flowers* Fully double, rosette, 1½in (4cm) across, borne in large, open, slightly drooping clusters. Creamy-white, opening from red buds. *Scent* Delicate, like primroses. *Leaves* Semi-evergreen, small, pointed. Dark green. *Blooming period* Midsummer.
• TIPS This vigorous, almost thornless rose has long been valued for its sweetly fragrant, rosette-form flowers, borne in swags and cascades in midsummer profusion. It is particularly effective if grown near still water where its reflection can be seen clearly. Since it performs·best with minimal pruning, it is also excellent for a pergola, arch, large tripod or pyramid, or for growing through trees. It tolerates poorer soils and light shade, and may be grown on a north or north-west facing wall.
• PARENTAGE Unknown.
• ORIGIN Jacques, France, 1827.
• OTHER NAMES 'Félicité et Perpétue'.

☼ ◊

Z 4–9

HEIGHT
15ft (5m)

SPREAD
12ft (4m)

Climber

ROSA 'Swan Lake'

Habit Upright, stiff, branching. *Flowers* Double, urn-shaped, 4in (10cm) across, singly, or in small clusters. White, tinted palest blush-pink at the center. *Scent* Light and sweet. *Leaves* Plentiful. Dark green. *Blooming period* Summer to autumn.
• TIPS Weather resistant, but may be prone to blackspot. A neatly growing climber for wall, fence, trellis or other support.
• PARENTAGE 'Memoriam' x 'Heidelberg'.
• ORIGIN McGredy, Northern Ireland, 1968.
• OTHER NAMES 'Schwanensee'.

Rambler

ROSA 'Goldfinch'

Habit Dense, arching, shrubby, almost thornless. *Flowers* Semi-double, rosette, 1½in (4cm) across, borne in large, neatly spaced clusters. Pale yolk-yellow, fading in hot sun to cream, showing golden stamens. *Scent* Strong and fruity. *Leaves* Plentiful, glossy. Mid-green. *Blooming period* Midsummer.
• TIPS Excellent for a wall, fence, pillar, or an old apple tree. Tolerates poorer soils and light shade. Attractive to bees.
• PARENTAGE 'Hélène' x unknown.
• ORIGIN Paul, England, 1907.

☼ ◊

Z 4–9

HEIGHT
10ft (3m)

SPREAD
6ft (1.8m)

☼ ◊

Z 4–9

HEIGHT
7ft (2.2m)

SPREAD
6ft (2m)

Climber

ROSA 'Mme. Alfred Carrière'

Habit Rather stiff, upright, with smooth, slender stems. *Flowers* Double, cupped, gardenia-like, 3in (8cm) across, in few-flowered clusters. Milky-white. *Scent* Fresh, sweet. *Leaves* Plentiful, large. Pale green. *Blooming period* Summer to autumn.
• TIPS Excellent for wall, tree, trellis, or pergola, or may be trained as a hedge. Very hardy and reliable, and tolerant of a north wall, though blooms less freely there.
• PARENTAGE Unknown.
• ORIGIN Schwartz, France, 1879.

Climber

ROSA 'New Dawn'

Habit Vigorous, arching, free-branching. *Flowers* Double, cupped, 3in (8cm) across, opening from pointed buds, in large sprays. Pale pearl-pink. *Scent* Sweet, fresh. *Leaves* Plentiful, semi-glossy. Rich green. *Blooming period* Midsummer to autumn.
• TIPS One of the easiest roses to grow on a pergola, arch, fence, wall, or pillar. Tolerates a north-facing wall. May be pruned as a hedge or shrub.
• PARENTAGE A sport of 'Dr. W. Van Fleet'.
• ORIGIN Somerset Rose Nurseries, US, 1930.
• OTHER NAMES 'Everblooming Dr. W. Van Fleet'.

☼ ◊

Z 4–9

HEIGHT
up to 18ft
(5.5m)

SPREAD
up to 10ft
(3m)

☼ ◊

Z 4–9

HEIGHT
up to 15ft
(5m)

SPREAD
up to 15ft
(5m)

Polyantha climber	

ROSA 'Climbing Cécile Brünner'

Habit Very vigorous. **Flowers** Fully double, urn-shaped, 1½in (4cm) across, opening from scrolled buds, borne singly, and in large well-spaced clusters. Pale shell-pink. **Scent** Delicate, fresh. **Leaves** Plentiful, dense. Bright green. **Blooming period** Repeating throughout summer.
• TIPS Suitable for growing through trees, clothing buildings, or for sturdy pergolas. Tolerates some shade. The flowers resemble those of its parent.
• PARENTAGE Sport of 'Cécile Brünner'.
• ORIGIN Hosp, US, 1894.

☼ ◊

Z 4–9

HEIGHT
to 25ft
(7.5m)

SPREAD
to 20ft (6m)

Rambler	

ROSA 'Little Rambler'

Habit Lax, spreading, with flexible stems. **Flowers** Fully double, rosette, 2in (5cm) across, in clusters along stems. Palest blush-pink. **Scent** Pervasive, sweet. **Leaves** Plentiful, small, semi-glossy. Dark green. **Blooming period** From summer to autumn.
• TIPS Excellent in a small garden or where space is confined, on a low fence, trellis, or pillar.
• PARENTAGE ('Cécile Brünner' x 'Baby Faurax') x ('Marjorie Fair' x 'Nozomi').
• ORIGIN Warner, England, 1994.
• OTHER NAMES 'Chewramb'.

☼ ◊

Z 4–9

HEIGHT
7ft (2.2m)

SPREAD
7ft (2.2m)

Rambler	

ROSA 'Blush Rambler'

Habit Vigorous, arching. **Flowers** Semi-double, cupped, 1½in (4cm) across, borne in large, conical, cascading clusters. Apple-blossom-pink, with golden stamens. **Scent** Light, delicate, and sweet. **Leaves** Plentiful. Light green. **Blooming period** In midsummer, but rather late.
• TIPS Tolerates poorer soils and partial shade. Excellent for a cottage garden, beautiful on a wall, pergola, or when grown through a tree.
• PARENTAGE 'Crimson Rambler' x 'The Garland'.
• ORIGIN Cant, England, 1903.

☼ ◊

Z 4–9

HEIGHT
9ft (2.8m)

SPREAD
12ft (4m)

Rambler	

ROSA 'Albertine'

Habit Vigorous, bushy with arching, branching, thorny, reddish stems. **Flowers** Fully double, cupped 3in (8cm) across, in small clusters. Coppery-pink, with salmon-red buds. **Scent** Rich, sweet. **Leaves** Plentiful, small, thick. Mid- to dark green. **Blooming period** Over a few weeks in midsummer.
• TIPS Excellent for a fence or pergola, or may be allowed to form a broad, sprawling shrub. Prone to mildew in dry conditions.
• PARENTAGE R. wichuraiana 'Mrs. A.R. Waddell'.
• ORIGIN Barbier, France, 1921.

☼ ◊

Z 5–9

HEIGHT
15ft (5m)

SPREAD
15ft (5m)

Climber	

ROSA 'Phyllis Bide'

Habit Vigorous, rather lax, freely branching.
Flowers Double, flat, 2in (5cm) across, opening
with conical hearts, borne in dainty clusters. Fawn,
flushed with pink and red, darkening with age.
Scent Little. *Leaves* Plentiful, with narrow,
glossy leaflets. Light green. *Blooming period*
Repeating throughout summer and autumn.
• TIPS Excellent on a wall, arch, and an ideal pillar
rose, since it seldom grows so vigorously that it
outgrows its allotted space. Usually remains
clothed almost to the base with bloom. This
dainty-flowered rose is nearly always best grown as
an isolated specimen where it can be appreciated
without competition from other, more showy
specimens. It tolerates poorer soils and light shade.
• PARENTAGE Thought to be 'Perle d'Or' x
'William Allen Richardson' or 'Gloire de Dijon'.
• ORIGIN Bide, England, 1923.

☀ ◌

Z 4–9

HEIGHT
8ft (2.5m)

SPREAD
5ft (1.5m)

Rambler	

ROSA 'Paul's Himalayan Musk'

Habit Vigorous, with long, slender shoots. **Flowers** Fully double, rosette, 1½in (4cm) across, on thread-like stems, in airy sprays. Blush- to lilac-pink, **Scent** Light, sweet. **Leaves** Long, drooping, pointed. Light green. **Blooming period** Once in midsummer.
• TIPS A rampant grower, suitable for a substantial pergola or large tree, especially in a wild garden.
• PARENTAGE Possibly *R. brunonii* x a Moschata hybrid.
• ORIGIN Attributed to Paul, England, 1916.
• OTHER NAMES 'Paul's Himalayan Rambler'.

☼ ◊

Z 4–9

HEIGHT
30ft (10m)

SPREAD
30ft (10m)

Climber	

ROSA 'High Hopes'

Habit Vigorous, upright, arching. **Flowers** Double, urn-shaped, 3–4in (8–10cm) across. Light rose-pink. **Scent** Sweet and moderately strong. **Leaves** Plentiful, glossy. Mid-green, flushed bronze. **Blooming period** Summer to autumn.
• TIPS Flowers are good for cutting and buttonholes. Suitable for a wall, fence, or pillar. Excellent for arch or pergola.
• PARENTAGE 'Compassion' x 'Congratulations'.
• ORIGIN Harkness, England, 1992.
• OTHER NAMES 'Haryup'.

☼ ◊

Z 4–9

HEIGHT
10ft (3m)

SPREAD
7ft (2.2m)

Climber	

ROSA 'Nice Day'

Habit Neat, upright, well-branched. **Flowers** Double, cupped, 2in (5cm) across, in clusters. Peach-pink. **Scent** Light, sweet. **Leaves** Plentiful, glossy. Mid-green, bronze-tinted. **Blooming period** Summer to autumn.
• TIPS Suitable for a low wall and for disguising unsightly corners in smaller gardens. Flowers are excellent for cutting or for buttonholes.
• PARENTAGE 'Sea Spray' x 'Warm Welcome'.
• ORIGIN Warner, England, 1994.
• OTHER NAMES 'Chewsea', 'Patio Queen'.

☼ ◊

Z 4–9

HEIGHT
7ft (2.2m)

SPREAD
3ft (1m)

Climber

ROSA 'Compassion'

Habit Sturdy, bushy, stiff, branching. **Flowers** Double, rounded, 4in (10cm) across, singly and in clusters. Rosy salmon-pink, with apricot tints. **Scent** Rich, strong, and sweet. **Leaves** Plentiful, large, very glossy. Dark green. **Blooming period** Repeats freely from summer to autumn.
• TIPS Especially suited for a wall, fence, or pillar in smaller gardens. May be pruned as a shrub.
• PARENTAGE 'White Cockade' x 'Prima Ballerina'.
• ORIGIN Harkness, England, 1973.
• OTHER NAMES 'Belle de Londres'.

☼ ◊
Z 4–9
HEIGHT 10ft (3m)
SPREAD 8ft (2.5m)

Climber

ROSA 'Mme. Grégoire Staechelin'

Habit Vigorous, arching. **Flowers** Fully double rounded to cupped, 5in (13cm) across, with ruffled petals, in large clusters. Clear pink, shaded carmine. **Scent** Like sweet peas. **Fruits** Large, red. **Leaves** Matte. Dark green. **Blooming period** Early summer.
• TIPS Good for a pergola, and excellent if trained horizontally on an extensive wall.
• PARENTAGE 'Frau Karl Druschki' x 'Château de Clos Vougeot'.
• ORIGIN Dot, Spain, 1927.
• OTHER NAMES 'Spanish Beauty'.

☼ ◊
Z 4–9
HEIGHT 20ft (6m)
SPREAD 12ft (4m)

Climber

ROSA 'Handel'

Habit Vigorous, stiffly upright, branching. **Flowers** Double, urn-shaped, 3–4in (8–10cm) across. Cream, edged with rose-pink. **Scent** Light, delicate. **Leaves** Glossy. Dark green, flushed bronze. **Blooming period** Midsummer, with lesser flushes to autumn.
• TIPS Good for a wall or pillar. May be pruned and grown as a shrub. Excellent for buttonholes. Occasionally suffers from blackspot.
• PARENTAGE 'Columbine' x 'Heidelberg'.
• ORIGIN McGredy, Northern Ireland, 1965.
• OTHER NAMES 'Macha'.

☼ ◊
Z 4–9
HEIGHT 10ft (3m)
SPREAD 7ft (2.2m)

Rambler

ROSA 'Veilchenblau'

Habit Vigorous, arching. **Flowers** Semi-double, rosette, 1in (2.5cm) across, in long-stemmed clusters. Violet with white centers and yellow stamens, aging to lilac-gray. **Scent** Fruity. **Leaves** Glossy. Light green. **Blooming period** Midsummer.
• TIPS Tolerates light shade. Suitable for a wall, arch, or pillar, and may be grown through smaller trees.
• PARENTAGE 'Crimson Rambler' x 'Erinnerung an Brod'.
• ORIGIN Schmidt, Germany, 1909.
• OTHER NAMES 'Blue Rambler', 'Violet Blue'.

☼ ◊
Z 4–9
HEIGHT 12ft (4m)
SPREAD 7ft (2.2m)

Climber	

ROSA 'Aloha'

Habit Sturdy, arching, rather slow-growing.
Flowers Fully double, deeply cupped, 3½in (9cm)
across. Rose-pink, with coppery-pink tones, and a
darker petal reverse. **Scent** Strong, sweet, and
pervasive. **Leaves** Plentiful, leathery. Dark green,
bronze-tinted. **Blooming period** Summer to autumn
• TIPS Suitable for a pillar, low wall, for a large
container, or may be grown as an arching shrub.
Good for cutting. Best with light pruning.
• PARENTAGE 'Mercedes Gallart' x 'New Dawn'.
• ORIGIN Boerner, US, 1949.

☼ ◊

Z 5–9

HEIGHT
8ft (2.5m)
or more

SPREAD
8ft (2.5m)

Climber	

ROSA 'Leaping Salmon'

Habit Stiff, well-branched. **Flowers** Double, urn-
shaped, 5in (12cm) across, opening from scrolled,
pointed buds. Soft salmon-pink. **Scent** Strong and
sweet. **Leaves** Glossy. Dark green. **Blooming
period** Summer to autumn.
• TIPS Flowers are excellent for cutting. Suitable
for a wall or fence.
• PARENTAGE [('Vesper' x 'Aloha') x ('Paddy
McGredy' x 'Maigold')] x 'Ballerina'.
• ORIGIN Pearce, England, 1986.
• OTHER NAMES 'Peamight'.

☼ ◊

Z 4–9

HEIGHT
10ft (3m)

SPREAD
6ft (1.8m)

Climber	

ROSA 'Lavinia'

Habit Shrubby, well-branched, stiff, upright.
Flowers Double, cupped, 5in (12cm) across,
borne singly, and in large clusters. Clear rose-pink.
Scent Sweet. **Leaves** Plentiful, glossy. Dark
green. **Blooming period** Repeating from summer
to autumn.
• TIPS Suitable for a warm wall, or may be
pruned as a shrub.
• PARENTAGE Not disclosed.
• ORIGIN Tantau, Germany, 1980.
• OTHER NAMES 'Tanklewi'.

☼ ◊

Z 4–9

HEIGHT
12ft (3.6m)

SPREAD
8ft (2.5m)

Climber	

ROSA 'Summer Wine'

Habit Upright, stiff, branching. **Flowers** Semi-
double, cupped, 4–5in (10–12cm) across, borne
singly, or in small clusters. Coral-pink, shaded
yellow at the base, with dark red-gold stamens,
Scent Slight. **Leaves** Large, semi-glossy.
Mid-green. **Blooming period** Summer to autumn.
• TIPS Hardy, healthy, and reliable. Good for a fence,
trellis, or pillar; effective against a pale background.
• PARENTAGE ' Coral Dawn' x seedling.
• ORIGIN Kordes, Germany, 1985.
• OTHER NAMES 'Korizont'.

☼ ◊

Z 4–9

HEIGHT
10ft (3m)

SPREAD
7ft (2.2m)

Climber	

ROSA 'Pink Perpétué'

Habit Vigorous, stiffly branched. **Flowers**
Double, cupped to rosette, 3in (8cm) across,
borne in large clusters. Clear pink, darker at the
base and on the petal reverse. **Scent** Light.
Leaves Plentiful, leathery. Glossy green.
Blooming period Repeating throughout
summer and autumn.
• TIPS Best in an open site, on a wall, fence,
or pillar. May also be pruned as a shrub.
• PARENTAGE 'Danse du Feu' x 'New Dawn'.
• ORIGIN Gregory, England, 1965.

Climber	

ROSA 'Climbing Mrs. Sam McGredy'

Habit Vigorous, stiff, well-branched. **Flowers**
Double, pointed, 5in (12cm) across. Deep salmon-
pink with coppery-red shadings. **Scent** Light and
sweet. **Leaves** Glossy. Dark green, mahogany-
tinted when young. **Blooming period** Repeating
from summer to autumn.
• TIPS Weather resistant. Prefers fertile soil and a
site sheltered from cold winds. Best against a wall,
where other plants obscure bare lower stems.
• PARENTAGE Sport of 'Mrs. Sam McGredy'.
• ORIGIN Buisman, Netherlands, 1937.

☼ ◊

Z 4–9

HEIGHT
10ft (3m)

SPREAD
8ft (2.5m)

☼ ◊

Z 4–9

HEIGHT
10ft (3m)

SPREAD
10ft (3m)

Climber	THORNLESS ROSE

ROSA 'Zéphirine Drouhin'

Habit Lax, arching, virtually thornless. **Flowers**
Double, cupped, 3in (8cm) across, in abundant
open clusters. Deep cerise-carmine pink. **Scent**
Sweet and rich. **Leaves** Semi-glossy. Mid-green.
Blooming period Throughout summer and autumn.
• TIPS Prone to mildew, but risk is reduced on a
west and north wall, where it can thrive. In sunnier
sites, grow on trellis, pillar, or fence to ensure good
air circulation. May be pruned as a shrub or hedge.
• PARENTAGE Unknown.
• ORIGIN Bizot, France, 1868 or 1873.

☼ ◊

Z 5–9

HEIGHT
8ft (2.5m)

SPREAD
6ft (2m)

Climber	

ROSA 'Climbing Orange Sunblaze'

Habit Upright, arching. **Flowers** Fully double, rosette, 1½in (4cm) across, borne in dense, many-flowered clusters. Brilliant orange-red. **Scent** Little. **Leaves** Plentiful, small, pointed, glossy. Dark green. **Blooming period** Summer to autumn.
• TIPS Excellent for confined spaces. Best in fertile soil and an open site.
• PARENTAGE Sport of 'Orange Sunblaze'.
• ORIGIN Meilland, France, 1986.
• OTHER NAMES 'Meijikatarsar'.

☼ ◊

Z 4–9

HEIGHT
5ft (1.5m)

SPREAD
28in (70cm)

Climber	

ROSA 'Morning Jewel'

Habit Vigorous, well-branched. **Flowers** Double, cupped, 3½in (9cm) across, in large and abundant clusters. Bright deep pink. **Scent** Sweet and fresh. **Leaves** Plentiful, very glossy. Dark green. **Blooming period** Prolific in midsummer, repeating later in the season.
• TIPS Disease and weather resistant. Suitable for walls, fences, and pillars. May also be pruned as a shrub.
• PARENTAGE 'New Dawn' x 'Red Dandy'.
• ORIGIN Cocker, Scotland, 1968.

☼ ◊

Z 4–9

HEIGHT
12ft (3.6m)

SPREAD
8ft (2.4m)

Rambler	

ROSA 'Dorothy Perkins'

Habit Vigorous, lax, with long, flexible stems. **Flowers** Double rosette, 1½in (4cm) across, borne in large, dense clusters. Clear, matte rose-pink. **Scent** Little. **Leaves** Plentiful, small, glossy. Mid- to dark green. **Blooming period** Midsummer.
• TIPS Susceptible to mildew, and best in moist but well-drained soil. Suitable for pillar, pergola, or arch, where air circulation is good. May also be grown as a weeping standard.
• PARENTAGE R. wichuraiana x 'Mme. Gabriel Luizet'.
• ORIGIN Jackson and Perkins, US, 1901.

☼ ◊

Z 4–9

HEIGHT
11ft (3.5m)

SPREAD
10ft (3m)

Climber	

ROSA 'Ramona'

Habit Vigorous, stiff, open, well-branched. **Flowers** Single, flat, 4in (10cm) across. Deep cerise-pink, with a grayish-pink petal reverse, and prominent golden stamens. **Scent** Little. **Leaves** Rather sparse, glossy. Dark green. **Blooming period** Early to midsummer only.
• TIPS Best against a warm, sheltered wall.
• PARENTAGE Sport of 'Anemone' (probably R. laevigata x a Tea Rose).
• ORIGIN Dietrich and Turner, US, 1913.
• OTHER NAMES 'Red Cherokee'.

☼ ◊

Z 4–9

HEIGHT
8ft (2.5m)

SPREAD
10ft (3m)

Climber

ROSA 'American Pillar'

Habit Robust, arching. **Flowers** Single, 2in (5cm) across, borne in showy, many-flowered clusters. Carmine-pink with a white eye. **Scent** None. **Leaves** Tough, glossy. Dark green. **Blooming period** Midsummer.
- TIPS Excellent for pillars, pergolas, or for growing into trees. Tolerates poorer soils and some shade.
- PARENTAGE (*R. wichuraiana* x *R. setigera*) x a red Hybrid Perpetual.
- ORIGIN Van Fleet, US, 1902.

Rambler

ROSA 'Crimson Shower'

Habit Vigorous, with long, flexible stems. **Flowers** Double, rosette, 1¼in (3cm) across, borne in large, dense, and very showy clusters. Deep crimson. **Scent** Light honey. **Leaves** Plentiful, with small, very shiny leaflets. Mid-green. **Blooming period** Late in midsummer to autumn.
- TIPS Suitable for a fence; ideal as a pillar, and excellent as a weeping standard.
- PARENTAGE Excelsa seedling.
- ORIGIN Norman, England, 1951.

☼ ◊

Z 4–9

HEIGHT
12ft (4m)

SPREAD
10ft (3m)

☼ ◊

Z 4–9

HEIGHT
8ft (2.5m)

SPREAD
7ft (2.2m)

Climber

ROSA 'Rosy Mantle'

Habit Vigorous, stiff, open-branched. **Flowers** Fully double, high-centered, 4in (10cm) across, opening from pointed buds. Rosy salmon-pink. **Scent** Rich and sweet. **Leaves** Glossy. Dark green. **Blooming period** Repeating throughout summer and autumn.
- TIPS Good for cutting, and suitable for a wall in the smaller garden.
- PARENTAGE 'New Dawn' x 'Prima Ballerina'.
- ORIGIN Cocker, Scotland, 1968.

Climber

ROSA 'Sympathie'

Habit Vigorous, well-branched. **Flowers** Fully double, deeply cupped, 3–4in (8–10cm) across, borne in wide-spaced clusters. Rich, bright blood-red. **Scent** Little. **Leaves** Plentiful, large, glossy, dark green. **Blooming period** Intermittently throughout summer and autumn.
- TIPS Hardy and reliable. Suitable for wall, pergola, trellis, or fence. Flowers are good for cutting.
- PARENTAGE 'Wilhelm Hansmann' x 'Don Juan'.
- ORIGIN Kordes, Germany, 1964.

☼ ◊

Z 4–9

HEIGHT
8ft (2.5m)

SPREAD
6ft (2m)

☼ ◊

Z 4–9

HEIGHT
10ft (3m)
or more

SPREAD
8ft (2.5m)

Climber	

ROSA 'Parkdirektor Riggers'

Habit Stiff, vigorous, well-branched. **Flowers**
Semi-double, 2½in (6cm) across, slightly cupped,
borne in large, many-flowered clusters. Velvety
dark crimson. **Scent** Little. **Leaves** Glossy, dark
green. **Blooming period** Repeating throughout
summer and autumn.

• TIPS This hardy, vigorous rose is justifiably
popular, producing a profusion of velvety crimson
flowers in repeat flushes throughout summer, set
against a backdrop of dark glossy foliage. It thrives,
and remains disease resistant in a variety of

situations; easy to grow. It is suitable for training
against a high wall, fence, or pillar, and
for pergolas. Roses of similar breeding that
have similar attributes and versatility include:
R. 'Leverkusen', with rosette-form, creamy-
yellow flowers, and R. 'Dortmund', with single,
crimson, white-eyed flowers.

• PARENTAGE R. x kordesii x 'Our Princess'.

• ORIGIN Kordes, Germany, 1957.

☼ ◊

Z 4–9

HEIGHT
12ft (3.6m)

SPREAD
8ft (2.5m)

Rambler	

ROSA 'Excelsa'

Habit Lax and flexible. **Flowers** Double, rosette, 1½in (4cm) across, borne in large, dense clusters. Crimson. **Scent** Little. **Leaves** Plentiful, small, shiny. Bright green. **Blooming period** Midsummer.
• TIPS Prone to mildew. Tolerates poorer soils and light shade. Suitable for pergola or tree. May also be grown as a weeping standard, or allowed to sprawl over a sunny bank.
• PARENTAGE Unknown.
• ORIGIN Walsh, US, 1909.
• OTHER NAMES 'Red Dorothy Perkins'.

☼ ◊

Z 4–9

HEIGHT
12ft (3.5m)

SPREAD
10ft (3m)

Climber	

ROSA 'Dortmund'

Habit Vigorous, upright. **Flowers** Single, flat, up to 4in (10cm) across, opening from long, slender buds, borne in dense, showy clusters. Bright red with a white eye. **Scent** Little. **Leaves** Very attractive, healthy, glossy. Dark green. **Blooming period** Repeating very freely from summer to autumn, if regularly deadheaded.
• TIPS Tolerates poorer soils. Suitable for a pillar, wall, or hedging. May be pruned as a shrub.
• PARENTAGE Seedling x R. x kordesii.
• ORIGIN Kordes, Germany, 1955.

☼ ◊

Z 4–9

HEIGHT
10ft (3m)

SPREAD
6ft (1.8m)

Climber	

ROSA 'Altissimo'

Habit Stiff, and sturdy. **Flowers** Single, flat, 5in (12cm) across, with neatly rounded petals, borne singly, and in clusters. Deep, unfading, bright red revealing golden stamens. **Scent** Little. **Leaves** Large, matte. Dark green. **Blooming period** Repeating from early summer.
• TIPS May be grown as a shrub, if pruned hard. Best in an open site. Suitable for a pillar or wall, but may clash with red brick.
• PARENTAGE Tenor seedling.
• ORIGIN Delbard-Chabert, France, 1966.

☼ ◊

Z 4–9

HEIGHT
10–12ft
(3–4m)

SPREAD
8ft (2.5m)

Climber	

ROSA 'Danse du Feu'

Habit Vigorous, stiffly branched. **Flowers** Double, rounded, 3in (8cm) across, borne in many-flowered clusters. Bright scarlet-red, aging crimson-purple. **Scent** Little. **Leaves** Plentiful, glossy. Dark green. **Blooming period** From summer to autumn.
• TIPS Suits moist but well-drained soil. Easily grown, but slightly susceptible to blackspot. Suitable for a wall, fence, or pillar.
• PARENTAGE 'Paul's Scarlet Climber' x R. multiflora.
• ORIGIN Mallerin, France, 1954.
• OTHER NAMES 'Spectacular'.

☼ ◊

Z 4–9

HEIGHT
8ft (2.5m)

SPREAD
8ft (2.5m)

Climber	

ROSA 'Dublin Bay'

Habit Dense, shrubby, free-flowering. **Flowers**
Double, cupped, 4in (10cm) across, borne in
clusters. Rich, bright, red-crimson. **Scent** Little.
Leaves Plentiful, large, very glossy. Mid-green.
Blooming period Repeating throughout summer
and autumn.
• TIPS Ideal for a pillar, but also grown as a shrub
or as an informal hedge. Well suited to smaller
gardens.
• PARENTAGE 'Bantry Bay' x 'Altissimo'.
• ORIGIN McGredy, New Zealand, 1976.

☼ ◊

Z 4–9

HEIGHT
7ft (2.2m)

SPREAD
7ft (2.2m)

Large-flowered climber	

ROSA 'Climbing Ena Harkness'

Habit Vigorous, stiff, well-branched. **Flowers**
Fully double, urn-shaped, velvety scarlet-
crimson, slender-stemmed, and nodding. **Scent**
Rich and sweet. **Leaves** Semi-glossy. Mid-green.
Blooming period Repeating from summer
to autumn.
• TIPS Suitable for a south- or west-facing wall or
pergola. Grows best in a warm, sunny, sheltered
site in fertile, moist, but well-drained soil.
• PARENTAGE Sport of 'Ena Harkness'.
• ORIGIN R. Murrell/ Gurteen and Ritson, 1954.

☼ ◊

Z 4–9

HEIGHT
15ft (4.5m)

SPREAD
8ft (2.5m)

Climber	

ROSA 'Guinée'

Habit Stiff, branching, vigorous. **Flowers** Fully
double, cupped, borne singly, or in small clusters.
Deepest crimson-maroon, velvety, scalloped petals,
opening almost flat to reveal golden stamens. **Scent**
Strong, rich, and sweet. **Leaves** Leathery. Dark
green. **Blooming period** Summer, sometimes with
a lesser flush in autumn.
• TIPS Best on a south- or west-facing wall or fence.
• PARENTAGE 'Souvenir de Claudius Denoyel' x
'Ami Quinard'.
• ORIGIN Mallerin, France, 1938.

☼ ◊

Z 4–9

HEIGHT
up to 15ft
(5m)

SPREAD
8ft (2.5m)

Climber	

ROSA 'Climbing Etoile de Hollande'

Habit Stiff, well-branched, rather open.
Flowers Double, deeply cupped, 5in (12cm)
across, produced in profusion. Rich deep crimson.
Scent Excellent, rich, heavy and pervasive.
Leaves Plentiful, matt. Dark green. **Blooming
period** From summer to autumn.
• TIPS Best on a large, warm, sunny wall or fence,
on fertile, moist, but well-drained soil.
• PARENTAGE Sport of 'Étoile de Hollande'.
• ORIGIN Leenders, The Netherlands, 1931.

☼ ◊

Z 4–9

HEIGHT
20ft (6m)

SPREAD
15ft (5m)

Climber	

ROSA 'Paul's Scarlet Climber'

Habit Upright, arching, vigorous, producing numerous shoots from the base. **Flowers** Semi-double, cupped, scarlet-crimson, borne in drooping, many-flowered clusters. **Scent** Little. **Leaves** Plentiful, matte. Dark green. **Blooming period** Midsummer.
• TIPS Hardy, reliable and free-flowering. Suitable for a pillar, pergola, fence, or wall. Tolerates poorer soils and light shade. Prone to mildew in dry sites.
• PARENTAGE Seedling of 'Paul's Carmine Pillar'.
• ORIGIN Paul, England, 1915.

☀ ◊

Z 4–9

HEIGHT
10ft (3m)

SPREAD
10ft (3m)

Large-flowered climber	

ROSA 'Paul's Lemon Pillar'

Habit Stiff, upright, branching. **Flowers** Double, large, pointed to rounded, 6in (15cm) across, drooping, and opening from scrolled buds. Creamy-lemon-white, flushed green at the base. **Scent** Refreshing and sweet. **Leaves** Large, rather sparse. Mid-green. **Blooming period** Midsummer only.
• TIPS Weather resistant, but best on a warm, sheltered wall. Despite the name, its stiff, branching habit is not well-suited to growing on a pillar.
• PARENTAGE 'Frau Karl Druschki' x 'Maréchal Niel'.
• ORIGIN Paul, England, 1915.

☀ ◊

Z 4–9

HEIGHT
15ft (5m) or more

SPREAD
10ft (3m)

Rambler	

R. 'Seagull'

Habit Vigorous, arching. **Flowers** Single to semi-double, 1½in (4cm) across, in large clusters. White, showing golden stamens. **Scent** Strong, sweet. **Leaves** Plentiful, with slender, pointed leaflets. Light grayish-green. **Blooming period** Summer.
• TIPS Excellent for a pergola or sturdy trellis. Similar in effect to R. 'Kiftsgate', but less vigorous and suitable for a smaller tree.
• PARENTAGE Said to be R. *multiflora* x 'Général Jacqueminot'.
• ORIGIN Pritchard, US, 1907.

☀ ◊

Z 4–9

HEIGHT
20ft (6m)

SPREAD
12ft (3.6m)

Climber	

ROSA 'Mermaid'

Habit Slow-growing, vigorous, stiff, branching.
Flowers Single, flat, 5in (12cm) across, in clusters.
Primrose-yellow, satiny, slightly waved petals with a
boss of amber-gold stamens. **Scent** Delicate, sweet.
Leaves Semi-evergreen, glossy. Dark green.
Blooming period Midsummer to autumn.
• TIPS Best in a sheltered site. Excellent for a sunny
wall. May be slow to establish. Resents pruning.
• PARENTAGE *R. bracteata* x a double yellow Tea
rose, perhaps 'Mme. de Tartas'.
• ORIGIN Paul, England, 1918.

☼ ◐

Z 4–9

HEIGHT
20ft (6m)

SPREAD
20ft (6m)

Climber	

ROSA 'Alister Stella Gray'

Habit Vigorous, upright, arching. **Flowers** Fully
double, quartered, 2½in (6cm) across, on long stems,
in sprays. Silky yellow petals, orange at base, fading
to creamy-white, opening from yolk-yellow buds.
Scent Rich, of tea. **Leaves** Dense, glossy. Dark
green. **Blooming period** Summer.
• TIPS Suitable for walls, arches, pergolas, pillars, or
for growing through trees. Best in a sheltered site.
• PARENTAGE Possibly a Noisette x a Tea rose.
• ORIGIN Gray, England, 1894.
• OTHER NAMES 'Golden Rambler'.

☼ ◐

Z 7–9

HEIGHT
15ft (4.5m)

SPREAD
10ft (3m)

Cluster-flowered climber	

ROSA 'Emily Gray'

Habit Arching with long flexible branches, with
sparse thorns. **Flowers** Semi-double, slightly
cupped, 3in (8cm) across, borne in small clusters.
Buff-yellow. **Scent** Light and sweet. **Leaves** Semi-
evergreen, plentiful, very glossy. Dark green, red-
tinted when young. **Blooming period** Midsummer.
• TIPS Suitable for a pergola, but best in a sheltered
yet open site, on a fence, or wall. May die back in
cold winters, and prone to mildew in dry conditions.
• PARENTAGE 'Jersey Beauty' x 'Comtesse du Cayla'.
• ORIGIN Williams, England, 1918.

☼ ◐

Z 4–9

HEIGHT
15ft (4.5m)

SPREAD
10ft (3m)

Climber	

ROSA 'Céline Forestier'

Habit Bushy, upright. **Flowers** Fully double,
neatly rounded, 5in (12cm) across, opening
quartered with a button eye, borne in few-flowered
clusters. Pale primrose-yellow. **Scent** Strong, spicy,
tea-rose fragrance. **Leaves** Plentiful. Light green.
Blooming period Repeating from spring to autumn.
• TIPS Slow to establish; rather tender, it performs
best on a warm, sunny, sheltered wall. May be
grown in containers or under glass.
• PARENTAGE Unknown.
• ORIGIN Trouillard, France, 1842.

☼ ◐

Z 7–9

HEIGHT
8ft (2.5m)
or more.

SPREAD
4ft (1.2m)

Rambler	

ROSA 'Wedding Day'

Habit Very vigorous, arching, clambering.
Flowers Single, flat, 1in (2.5cm) across, with well-spaced petals, in numerous, many-flowered clusters. Creamy-white aging to palest blush-pink. *Scent* Sweet and fruity. *Fruits* Small, oval hips. Yellow. *Leaves* Glossy. Bright green. *Blooming period* Mid- to late summer.
• TIPS Excellent for growing through a tree or for clothing unsightly buildings, especially in a wild or woodland garden. In these conditions the planting site, preferably on the sunny side of the tree or building, should be enriched with well-rotted manure or compost. It has an exceptional fragrance, although the wedge-shaped petals are unfortunately often spotted by rain.
• PARENTAGE Seedling of *R. sinowilsonii* (syn. *R. longicuspis* var. *sinowilsonii*).
• ORIGIN Stern, England, 1950.

☼ ◊

Z 4–9

HEIGHT
25ft (8m)

SPREAD
12ft (4m)

Climber	

ROSA 'Casino'

Habit Vigorous, stiff. *Flowers* Double, globular, 4in (10cm) across, opening to a flat, often quartered rosette from pointed buds, borne singly, and in clusters. Soft yellow. *Scent* Light and sweet. *Leaves* Glossy. Light green. *Blooming period* Repeating throughout summer.
• TIPS Suitable for walls, fences, and pillars, or may be grown as a shrub if pruned hard.
• PARENTAGE 'Coral Dawn' x 'Buccaneer'.
• ORIGIN McGredy, Northern Ireland, 1963.
• OTHER NAMES 'Gerbe d'Or', 'Macca'.

☼ ◊

Z 4–9

HEIGHT
10ft (3m)

SPREAD
7ft (2.2m)

Climber	

ROSA 'Laura Ford'

Habit Upright, well-branched. *Flowers* Semi-double, cupped, 2in (5cm) across, borne in dense clusters. Bright yellow, touched with pink. *Scent* Moderately sweet. *Leaves* Plentiful, small, glossy. Dark green. *Blooming period* Summer to autumn.
• TIPS Suitable for a low wall, fence, or pillar; ideal for smaller gardens.
• PARENTAGE 'Anna Ford' x ['Elizabeth of Glamis' x ('Galway Bay' x 'Sutter's Gold')].
• ORIGIN Warner, England, 1990.
• OTHER NAMES 'Chewarvel'.

☼ ◊

Z 4–9

HEIGHT
7ft (2.2m)

SPREAD
4ft (1.2m)

Climber	

ROSA 'Dreaming Spires'

Habit Upright, stiff, well branched. *Flowers* Double, rounded, 5in (12cm) across, borne singly, and in small clusters. Yellow, with a hint of orange. *Scent* Sweet and fresh. *Leaves* Plentiful. Dark bluish-green. *Blooming period* From summer to autumn.
• TIPS Good for a warm, sunny wall, pillar, or fence; especially attractive against a dark background.
• PARENTAGE 'Buccaneer' x 'Arthur Bell'.
• ORIGIN Mattock, England, 1973.

☼ ◊

Z 4–9

HEIGHT
10ft (3m)

SPREAD
7ft (2.2m)

Climber	

ROSA 'Golden Showers'

Habit Stiff, upright, branching. *Flowers* Loosely double, rounded, opening almost flat, 4in (10cm) across, with ruffled petals, in clusters. Deep golden-yellow, fading to creamy-yellow. *Scent* Light, sweet. *Leaves* Glossy. Dark green. *Blooming period* From summer into autumn with good continuity.
• TIPS Excellent for a wall or pillar, and, if pruned hard, may be grown as a shrub. Tolerates poorer soils and light shade. Needs minimal pruning as a climber.
• PARENTAGE 'Charlotte Armstrong' x 'Capt. Thomas'.
• ORIGIN Lammerts, US, 1957.

☼ ◊

Z 4–9

HEIGHT
up to 10ft
(3m)

SPREAD
7ft (2.2m)

Climber

ROSA 'Maigold'

Habit Vigorous, stiff, arching. *Flowers* Semi-double, cupped, 4in (10cm) across, borne in clusters. Rich bronze-yellow. *Scent* Strong and sweet. *Leaves* Plentiful, leathery, glossy. Rich green. *Blooming period* In summer, with a few flowers later in the season.

• TIPS Tolerates a range of soils and conditions including poorer soils and light shade. While ideally suitable for walls and pergolas, it may also be grown as a shrub. The parents of this rose have passed on a very tough, hardy and disease resistant constitution, making it one of the best roses for exposed sites. It is valued for its free-flowering nature; the blooms are borne in great profusion, early in the season, and it is often one of the first of the roses to come into flower.

• PARENTAGE 'Poulsens Pink' x 'Frühlingstag'.
• ORIGIN Kordes, Germany, 1953.

☼: ◊

Z 4–9

HEIGHT
8ft (2.5m)

SPREAD
8ft (2.5m)

Climber	

ROSA 'Easlea's Golden Rambler'

Habit Vigorous, arching. *Flowers* Fully double, loosely formed, rounded, 5in (12cm) across, borne in small, long-stemmed clusters. Apricot-yellow, flecked with red. *Scent* Sweet. *Leaves* Leathery. Dark green. *Blooming period* Midsummer.
• TIPS Suitable for a pergola, and good for cutting. Tolerates poorer soils and light shade.
• PARENTAGE Unknown.
• ORIGIN Easlea, England, 1932.

☼ ◊

Z 4–9

HEIGHT
20ft (6m)

SPREAD
15ft (4.5m)

Climber	BANKSIAN YELLOW, YELLOW BANKSIAN

ROSA BANKSIAE 'Lutea'

Habit Very vigorous, arching, graceful, usually almost thornless. *Flowers* Fully double, rosette, ¾in (2cm) across, borne in pendent clusters. Clear, light yellow. *Scent* Little. *Leaves* Smooth with small, long, pointed leaflets. Light green.
Blooming period Late spring or early summer, in profusion.
• TIPS The hardiest of the Banksian roses. Needs minimal pruning; flowers are produced on second and third year wood.
• ORIGIN China, introduced to Europe, 1824.

☼ ◊

Z 7–9

HEIGHT
to 30ft
(10m)

SPREAD
to 30ft
(10m)

Climber	

ROSA 'Good as Gold'

Habit Dense, stiff, branching. *Flowers* Double, urn-shaped, 2–3in (5–8cm) across, borne in large clusters. Golden-yellow. *Scent* Sweet and fresh. *Leaves* Small, narrow, glossy. Dark green. *Blooming period* Summer to autumn with excellent continuity.
• TIPS Good for cutting. Suitable for a low wall, fence, or pillar; ideal for smaller gardens.
• PARENTAGE 'Anne Harkness' × 'Laura Ford'.
• ORIGIN Warner, England, 1995
• OTHER NAMES 'Chewsunbeam'.

☼ ◊

Z 4–9

HEIGHT
6ft (2m)

SPREAD
5ft (1.5m)

Climber	

ROSA 'Climbing Lady Hillingdon'

Habit Stiff, well-branched. **Flowers** Nodding, semi-double, cupped, to 6in (15cm) across, borne in open sprays. Light apricot-yellow, opening from slender, pointed, coppery-apricot buds. **Scent** Rich, fruity, tea-scented. **Leaves** Glossy. Dark grayish green, tinted mahogany and purple on emergence. **Blooming period** Repeats from summer to autumn.
• TIPS Flowers are good for cutting. Best in a warm, sheltered site.
• PARENTAGE Sport of 'Lady Hillingdon' bush rose.
• ORIGIN Hicks, England, 1917.

☼: ◐

Z 4–9

HEIGHT
15ft (4.5m)

SPREAD
8ft (2.5m)

Climber	

ROSA 'Night Light'

Habit Stiff, well-branched. **Flowers** Double, pointed, with rounded outline, 5in (12cm) across. Deep yellow, aging orange-yellow, opening from pointed, red-tinted buds. **Scent** Light and sweet. **Leaves** Plentiful, glossy. Dark green. **Blooming period** Summer to autumn.
• TIPS Suitable for a wall, fence, or pillar.
• PARENTAGE 'Westerland' x 'Pastorale'.
• ORIGIN Poulsen, Denmark, 1982.
• OTHER NAMES 'Poullight', 'Night Life'.

☼: ◐

Z 4–9

HEIGHT
8ft (2.5m)

SPREAD
7ft (2.2m)

Climber	

ROSA 'Della Balfour'

Habit Vigorous, upright, stiff. **Flowers** Double, high-centered, 4in (10cm) across, borne singly, or in clusters. Orange with salmon-pink. **Scent** Refreshing, lemony. **Leaves** Plentiful, leathery. Dark green. **Blooming period** From summer to autumn.
• TIPS Ideal for wall, fence, and pillar.
• PARENTAGE 'Rosemary Harkness' x 'Elina'.
• ORIGIN Harkness, England, 1994
• OTHER NAMES 'Harblend'.

☼: ◐

Z 4–9

HEIGHT
8ft (2.5m)

SPREAD
6ft (1.8m)

Climber	OLD GLORY ROSE

ROSA 'Gloire de Dijon'

Habit Vigorous, stiff, branching. **Flowers** Full double, quartered-rosette, 4in (10cm) across. Deep buff-yellow, with amber and pink tints, more pink in warm weather. **Scent** Sweet and pervasive. **Leaves** Semi-glossy. Mid- to light green, red-tinted when young. **Blooming period** Repeats from early summer to autumn.
• TIPS Excellent for a warm, sunny wall.
• PARENTAGE Unknown Tea rose x 'Souvenir de la Malmaison'.
• ORIGIN Jacotot, France, 1853.

☼: ◐

Z 7–9

HEIGHT
15ft (4.5m)

SPREAD
12ft (4m)

Cluster-flowered climber/shrub	

ROSA 'City Girl'

Habit Vigorous, freely branching. **Flowers** Semi-double, opening cupped, from pointed buds, 4½in (11cm) across, in large, showy clusters. Salmon-pink. **Scent** Refreshing and spicy. **Leaves** Plentiful, glossy. Dark green. **Blooming period** Freely from summer to autumn.
• TIPS Excellent for a wall, fence, or pergola. May be grown unpruned as a large, shrubby specimen plant. Valued for its showy clusters of attractively formed flowers, this rose has a good scent and is best planted close to the house to frame a doorway, porch, or window where its fragrance can be appreciated at close quarters.
• PARENTAGE 'Compassion' x 'Armada'.
• ORIGIN Harkness, England, 1994.
• OTHER NAMES 'Harzorba'.

☼ ◊

Z 4–9

HEIGHT
8ft (2.5m)

SPREAD
8ft (2.5m)

Climber	

ROSA 'Schoolgirl'

Habit Stiff, upright, rather lanky. *Flowers* Fully double, urn-shaped to rounded, 4in (10cm) across,. Warm, deep apricot. *Scent* Rich and sweet. *Leaves* Rather sparse, large. Dark green. *Blooming period* Summer to autumn.
• TIPS Suitable for a wall or trellis. Best in a sunny, sheltered site.
• PARENTAGE 'Coral Dawn' x 'Belle Blonde'.
• ORIGIN McGredy, Northern Ireland, 1964.

☼ ◊

Z 4–9

HEIGHT
9ft (2.8m)

SPREAD
7ft (2.2m)

Climber	

ROSA 'Breath of Life'

Habit Stiffly upright. *Flowers* Fully double, rounded, 4in (10cm) across. Apricot, aging with pink tones. *Scent* Sweet and fresh. *Leaves* Semi-glossy. Mid-green. *Blooming period* From summer to autumn.
• TIPS Suitable for a wall, fence, or pillar; if pruned hard, it may be grown as a shrub. Flowers are good for cutting.
• PARENTAGE 'Red Dandy' x 'Alexander'.
• ORIGIN Harkness, England, 1982.
• OTHER NAMES 'Harquanne'.

☼ ◊

Z 4–9

HEIGHT
9ft (2.8m)

SPREAD
7ft (2.2m)

Climber	

ROSA 'Meg'

Habit Vigorous and stiff. *Flowers* Semi-double, 5in (12cm) across, in small clusters. Wavy, apricot-pink petals surrounding dark golden stamens. *Scent* Rich, sweet. *Leaves* Plentiful, large. Dark green. *Blooming period* Summer to autumn.
• TIPS Suitable for a wall, high fence, or pergola; it may be allowed to scramble through other robust shrubs or hedging.
• PARENTAGE Probably 'Paul's Lemon Pillar' x 'Madame Butterfly'.
• ORIGIN Gosset, England, 1954.

☼ ◊

Z 4–9

HEIGHT
12ft (3.6m)

SPREAD
12ft (3.6m)

Climber	

ROSA 'Warm Welcome'

Habit Upright, arching, free-branching. *Flowers* Semi double, cupped, 2in (5cm) across, in clusters. Orange-vermilion, flushed yellow at the base. *Scent* Little. *Leaves* Plentiful. Dark green. *Blooming period* Summer to autumn, with good continuity.
• TIPS Weather and disease resistant. Suitable for a wall, fence, or pillar, especially in confined spaces.
• PARENTAGE ['Elizabeth of Glamis'. x ('Galway Bay' x 'Sutters Gold')] x 'Anna Ford'.
• ORIGIN Warner, England, 1991.
• OTHER NAMES 'Chewizz'.

☼ ◊

Z 4–9

HEIGHT
7ft (2.2m)

SPREAD
7ft (2.2m)

CARING FOR ROSES

Despite the enormous diversity within the group, roses are not difficult to grow provided that their basic needs are met. The majority are long-lived, and attention paid to choosing a suitable site, good soil preparation, and selecting appropriate cultivars will be amply rewarded for years to come.

Roses can be purchased bare-rooted or container-grown; both should have at least two strong stems, with a healthy network of roots in proportion to the top-growth. The foliage of container-grown plants should be well-balanced, healthy, and free of symptoms of pests or diseases. Standard roses should have a balanced head and a reasonably straight stem, free of obvious kinks.

Bare-root roses are sold in a dormant or semi-dormant state with their roots packed in compost or clean of soil. Look for a good network of fibrous roots and a strong union where the top-growth joins the rootstock. Do not buy plants whose roots show any signs of drying out, or if growth buds have begun to sprout. This may indicate that they have been badly stored in warm, dry conditions, and such neglected specimens seldom establish well.

Examine a container-grown rose carefully before buying. Check that is firmly rooted; if not, it may be an unsold and recently potted bare-root rose whose root system has been exposed to the elements during dormancy. A container-grown rose should have a network of healthy roots that almost fill the pot. Reject plants with coiled, congested, or pot-bound roots, as they may have suffered nutrient deficiencies or other damage from being in pots too long.

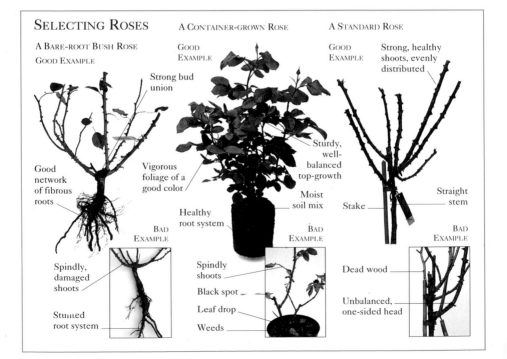

SELECTING ROSES

A BARE-ROOT BUSH ROSE
GOOD EXAMPLE

Strong bud union

Good network of fibrous roots

Vigorous foliage of a good color

BAD EXAMPLE

Spindly, damaged shoots

Stunted root system

A CONTAINER-GROWN ROSE

GOOD EXAMPLE

Healthy root system

Sturdy, well-balanced top-growth

Moist soil mix

BAD EXAMPLE

Spindly shoots

Black spot

Leaf drop

Weeds

A STANDARD ROSE

GOOD EXAMPLE

Strong, healthy shoots, evenly distributed

Stake

Straight stem

BAD EXAMPLE

Dead wood

Unbalanced, one-sided head

SOIL PREPARATION AND PLANTING

Almost all roses grow best in full sun, with shelter from strong, cold winds and good air circulation. Most prefer a fertile, moist but well-drained, slightly acid soil, with a pH of about 6.5. The old garden roses are the most tolerant of alkaline soils, provided they are deeply cultivated and enriched with plentiful organic matter. The drainage, aeration, and moisture-holding properties of most soil types will be improved by the addition of well-rotted organic matter. Very wet soils can be improved by installing a drainage system, and soil acidity or alkalinity may be modified to some degree by liming very acid soils or by adding well-rotted organic matter to alkaline ones. All pre-planting

HOW TO PLANT A BARE-ROOT BUSH ROSE

1 *Remove dead, diseased, or damaged growth. Cut out crossing and spindly shoots at their base to leave a well-balanced framework of 3–5 shoots. Trim any thick roots by about one-third of their length.*

2 *Dig the planting hole in well-prepared soil and fork half a bucketful of compost, mixed with a handful of bone meal or balanced, slow-release fertilizer, into the bottom of the hole.*

3 *Set the rose in the hole and spread out the roots evenly. Check the depth by laying a stake across the top of the hole to ensure that the bud union will be about 1in (2.5cm) below the final soil level.*

4 *Backfill with soil, firming with the fingers and shaking gently to remove air pockets and ensure good contact between roots and soil. Firm surrounding soil lightly. Rake over and water in well.*

cultivation and incorporation of organic matter should be completed about three months before planting, to allow the soil to settle adequately.

New roses may not thrive in soil where roses have been grown before, since they are often affected by "rose-sickness"or "replant disease," a combination of soil-borne nematodes, viruses, and fungi that attacks the feeder roots of new roses, causing reduced vigor and poor establishment. The easiest and cheapest option is to site new roses where other roses have never been grown before, or where the border has been clear of roses for several years. If replanting only one or two roses in an established bed, dig a hole 24in (60cm) square, and 18in (45cm) deep, and replace the soil with virgin soil from another part of the garden. One or two chemical soil sterilizers are also now available commercially, although most still require the services of a professional.

When to plant
Plant bare-root roses during the dormant season in late autumn or early winter, or in early spring, as soon as possible after purchase. If planting is delayed, because of unsuitable soil or weather conditions for example, heel the plants into a shallow trench on a piece of spare

ground, or store them in a cool, frost-free place and keep the roots moist.

Container-grown roses may be planted at any time of year provided the soil is not frozen, nor too wet or dry. If they have to be left outdoors during very cold weather, the container should be covered to protect the roots.

Spacing and planting depths
The growth habit and size of a rose determines its appropriate planting distances. Planting too close together makes access for mulching, spraying, and pruning difficult and can create stagnant air conditions that permit rapid spread of blackspot or mildew. Roses of narrow, upright habit need less space than those with lax or arching growth. Plant bedding roses 18–24in (45–60cm) apart, and at least 12in (30cm) from the edge of the bed. Larger and more spreading roses need spacings of 2½–4ft (75–120cm) depending on their ultimate size, while miniature roses are planted at about 12in (30cm) apart. Rose hedges are planted in a single or staggered, double row to gain uniformly dense growth (see below). In general, plant grafted roses with the bud union about 1in (2.5cm) below soil level. Plant species roses and those on their own roots at the same depth as they were in the pot or open ground.

ROSE HEDGE PLANTING DISTANCES

Vigorous hedging roses
Plant tall, dense or spreading roses in a single line, 3–4ft (1–1.2m) apart, so that when the rose matures the branches interlace to form a dense and effective screen.

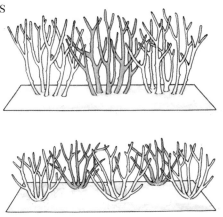

Modern bush roses
For shorter, more upright roses, plant in two rows in a double, staggered formation to produce dense coverage. The rows should be 18–24in (45–60cm) apart, and each plant should be 18–24in (45–60cm) from the next.

PLANTING A CLIMBING ROSE

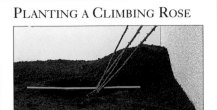

1 *Place the rose in a planting hole, about 18in (45cm) away from the wall. Set it at an angle of 45°, so that the shoots reach the lowest support wire. Use a stake to check planting depth.*

2 *Use stakes to guide shorter shoots to the supporting wires. Tie in all the shoots to the stakes or wires with clips (see inset). Loosen clips regularly as growth proceeds, to avoid constriction.*

How to plant

The basic planting technique is similar for all roses, but varies slightly for climbers and ramblers (see left) and for standard roses (p.136). First ensure that the roots are moist by watering the pot well, or by soaking bare-root roses for up to an hour before planting. Prune off any damaged or diseased roots and top-growth. Make a planting hole that is wide enough to accommodate the roots or root ball and deep enough for the bud union to sit 1in (2.5cm) below soil level. For non-grafted roses, the soil surface should be at the same level on the stem as it was in the pot or soil. Incorporate bone meal and compost into the bottom of the planting hole. Position the rose in the hole, spread the roots, and check the planting depth. If a bare-rooted rose has roots that grow in one direction, place the stem close to one side of the hole and spread the roots fan-wise, as widely as possible. Then backfill with soil, firming carefully as you go, shaking the plant gently to ensure good contact between the roots and soil. Tread the rose in firmly but gently, with the tip of the toe, taking care neither to damage the roots, nor to compact heavy or silty soil. Then label and water in thoroughly. Delay the application of a mulch until spring.

PLANTING ROSES IN CONTAINERS

Choose a container at least 12–18in (30–45cm) deep for bush roses and 9–14in (23–35cm) deep for miniatures. Place a small piece of mesh or screen in the bottom, and top with upside-down sod, to prevent the soil mix from washing through the drainage hole. Fill the pot with a good-quality, soil-based potting mix. Space correctly, and plant the roses in the same way, and at the correct depth, as for bush roses (p.133).

HOW TO PLANT A STANDARD ROSE

1 *All standard roses need a firm stake, placed on the side of the prevailing wind. Set the rose in the center of the hole, and drive the stake into the ground so that the top is just below the head of the rose.*

2 *Check the planting depth with a stake, and, using the old soil mark on the stem as a guide, plant at the same depth. The bud unions of standard roses are at the top and the bottom of the stem.*

3 *Use rose ties (see inset) to attach the rose to the stake. Put one at the top of the stake just below the head to give support, and one halfway up the stem. Cut out any weak or crossing shoots.*

ROUTINE CARE

If roses are to develop as healthy, vigorous plants, they need regular attention to feeding, mulching, and watering, as well as routine operations such as deadheading, weeding, and the removal of suckers (see right and below). Suckers may arise from below the graft union, and usually have markedly different leaf shape and color. They must be removed if they are not to out-compete the grafted cultivar.

Roses expend enormous energies in the production of growth and flowers, and most are gross feeders. Even on fertile soils they exhaust soil nutrients quickly, so fertilizer must be applied regularly to replenish them. Commercial rose fertilizers supply all major nutrients and trace elements, and are available in powder or granulated form. Following the manufacturer's instructions, apply fertilizer into moist soil around each plant, after pruning in spring. Then apply a 3in (8cm) mulch of well-rotted

SUCKERS ON A STANDARD ROSE

Pull away any suckers growing from the rose stem, taking care not to rip the bark. Alternatively cut off the sucker cleanly, and rub out any new buds that emerge around the wound as soon as seen.

REMOVING A SUCKER FROM A BUSH ROSE

1 *Suckers usually have leaves of different shape and color than the cultivar. Carefully scrape away the soil to reveal the top of the rootstock. Check that the suspect shoot arises from below the bud union.*

2 *Pull the sucker away sharply from the rootstock; this technique also removes any dormant sucker buds. Cutting off suckers merely stimulates these dormant buds to grow. Refill the hole and firm the soil.*

organic matter to reduce weed growth, conserve soil moisture, and maintain even soil temperatures. Make a second application of fertilizer about one month later to promote further flushes of bloom. Do not apply a balanced fertilizer late in the season; it promotes soft growth that is susceptible to damage by frosts. Instead, apply a high-potash fertilizer in early autumn, at a rate of 2oz/sq yd (75g/sq m), to help late shoots mature. Roses in containers need an annual top-dressing of balanced fertilizer in spring, followed by foliar feeds during the growing season to maintain vigorous growth.

Roses produce deep roots and, once established in well-prepared soil, seldom need additional watering, even in hot,

BLIND SHOOTS

Cut the blind shoot back by about a half to an outward-facing bud to encourage it to grow and flower. If no budding eye is visible, cut back to the main stem.

HOW TO DEADHEAD ROSES

Hybrid Tea
Cut the stems bearing faded flowers back to an outward-facing bud, or to a fully formed shoot bearing at least one full-sized leaf. Removing old flowers encourages the plant to produce new growth.

Floribunda
The central flower of the cluster fades first and is removed to maintain the display. When all the flowers have faded, remove the whole cluster by cutting back to an emerging bud or fully formed shoot.

CUTTING BACK IN AUTUMN

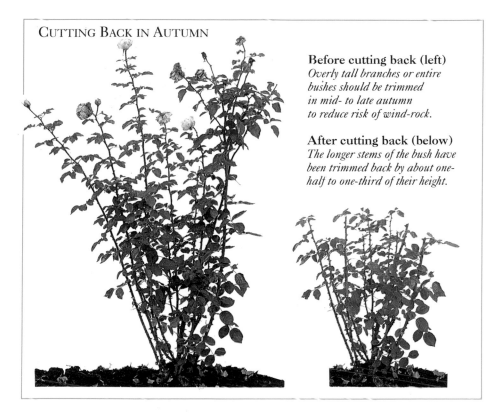

Before cutting back (left)
Overly tall branches or entire bushes should be trimmed in mid- to late autumn to reduce risk of wind-rock.

After cutting back (below)
The longer stems of the bush have been trimmed back by about one-half to one-third of their height.

dry summers. While they are becoming established, however, they should be watered regularly during dry periods. Soak each plant thoroughly, applying at least a bucketful of water to the immediate root area, preferably in the evenings when evaporation from the soil surface is reduced. Watering little and often merely encourages surface rooting, and surface roots are far more susceptible to heat and drought. Roses in containers need regular watering to keep the soil evenly moist, and in dry periods, they may need watering daily. During the growing season, observe plants regularly for signs of pests and disease. The most common problems include aphids, blackspot, powdery mildew, and rust. All are most easily controlled if treated in the early stages of infestation or infection, using an appropriate pesticide or fungicide. Good hygiene, including the removal of fallen leaves, prunings, and other debris, helps to control the spread of disease.

Deadheading and cutting back
Unless roses produce ornamental hips as well as flowers, they should be deadheaded as the blooms fade to prolong the flowering season (see left). If left in place, energy is diverted into the production of seed rather than new flowering shoots. If, on bush roses, blind or non-flowering shoots arise, these will continue to expend energy on vegetative growth at the expense of flowers unless removed (see above left).

Strong winter winds may loosen the roots of roses, thus making them liable to cold damage and drying out. To reduce the risk of wind-rock, shorten overly long top-growth or the entire plant in autumn.

PRUNING AND TRAINING

The primary aim when pruning roses is to produce the optimum display of blooms on an attractively shaped bush. Pruning helps to speed up the natural growth cycles whereby old, weak growth is replaced by vigorous new shoots that flower more freely. In climbing roses, pruning and training onto a support helps to promote the production of flowering sideshoots and directs new growth to fill the allotted space.

Pruning permits good air circulation, and induces the plant to concentrate energy into the growth of the remaining healthy shoots. A pair of sharp, high-quality pruners is essential, along with a pair of strong, protective gloves. Pruning saws and loppers are useful to cut thick stems and old woody stumps. First remove all dead, diseased, or damaged wood, cutting back into healthy white pith, even if this means cutting back to ground level. Then remove any crossing shoots and weak or spindly growth. Always make a clean cut just above a healthy bud, angled away from the direction in which the resultant shoot is

to develop, so that any moisture is shed away from the developing bud. Cuts are usually made to an outward-facing bud, but on roses of lax habit, it may be necessary to select an inward-facing one to fill up an open center.

In most cases, pruning is done when the plant is dormant or semi-dormant, between leaf-fall in autumn and bud-break in early spring. Do not prune in very cold weather, since the growth bud below the cut may be damaged, and the shoot may die back. If winters are severe, it will be necessary to cut cold-damaged shoots back again to a healthy bud in spring. Where severe winters are the norm, delay pruning until early spring. In warm climates, where temperatures seldom fall below freezing, roses may bloom almost continuously. To prevent them from becoming exhausted, prune in the cooler months to induce dormancy and give them an artificial period of rest.

Nearly all newly planted roses should be pruned back hard to within 3–6in (8–15cm) above ground level to encourage the development of a

MAKING A PRUNING CUT

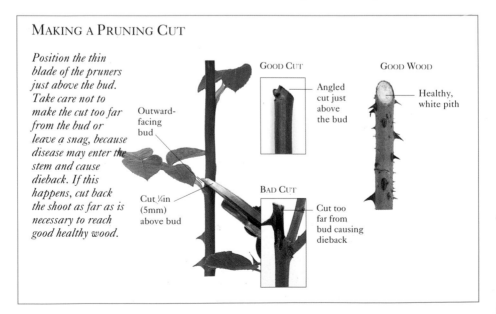

Position the thin blade of the pruners just above the bud. Take care not to make the cut too far from the bud or leave a snag, because disease may enter the stem and cause dieback. If this happens, cut back the shoot as far as is necessary to reach good healthy wood.

Outward-facing bud

Cut ¼in (5mm) above bud

GOOD CUT

Angled cut just above the bud

BAD CUT

Cut too far from bud causing dieback

GOOD WOOD

Healthy, white pith

How to Prune a Hybrid Tea

Prune main stems to within 8–24in (20–60cm) of ground level to form a strong, balanced framework.

In autumn or spring, cut out any crossing, congested, and spindly growth.

Remove dead wood and any that shows signs of damage or disease.

Pruning a Newly Planted Bush

Prune a newly planted bush rose to about 3–6in (8–15cm) above ground level. Remove weak or damaged growth, and cut back remaining strong stems to outward-facing buds.

well-balanced framework of sturdy, healthy shoots, and a strong root system.

Climbing roses are one exception to this rule. In their first one or two years, priority is given to training, and they are pruned only to remove dead, diseased, damaged, or spindly shoots. Roses grown as standards also need minimal pruning to remove dead, diseased, and damaged wood, along with any crossing or rubbing shoots that may cause congestion in the center of the head.

Pruning bush roses

Once established, the various groups of roses have different pruning needs to suit their habit, and to take account of the age of the flowering wood. Most modern roses bloom on the current year's wood and, if cut back when dormant, produce new shoots that bloom freely in the same year. Hard pruning generally produces larger, but fewer, blooms. Recent pruning trials of bush roses by Britain's Royal National Rose Society suggest that alternative pruning methods can yield results as good as or sometimes better than the traditional methods. In particular it has been shown that "rough-pruned" plants, pruned without regard to the location of the budding eyes, do not appear to be disadvantaged by dieback. It is also believed that the retention of some twiggy growth can be helpful, because these growths leaf out early in spring and the food·they provide enables the bushes to grow faster. The trials continue.

Hybrid Teas
(Large-flowered bush roses)
Prune when dormant. First remove dead, diseased, damaged, and weak growth (p.141). Use loppers to remove any old unproductive stumps left from previous prunings. Cut the remaining stems back hard to leave a balanced framework with an open center to permit air to circulate. In temperate climates, cut back main shoots to about 8–10in (20–25cm) above ground level, in milder areas prune less severely, to about 18–24in (45–60cm). To produce exhibition-quality blooms, the main stems are cut back to 2–3 buds.

Floribundas
(Cluster-flowered bush roses)
Prune when dormant. Cut unproductive wood away and prune back the main shoots of smaller cultivars to about 12–15in (30–38cm) above ground level and reduce sideshoots by one-third. Reduce main shoots of taller cultivars of 4ft (1.2m) or more, by about one-third of their height and cut back sideshoots by up to two-thirds. Use the same principles to prune dwarf cluster-flowered bushes.

HOW TO PRUNE A FLORIBUNDA

In autumn or spring, remove crossing or congested wood, and all twiggy or spindly growth.

Reduce sideshoots by one- to two-thirds, cutting back to a strong, healthy bud.

Prune out all dead, damaged, or diseased wood, cutting back to a healthy bud.

Prune the main shoots to about 12–32in (30–80cm) above ground level,

Miniature roses

These roses may be treated in one of two ways. The first method is to prune minimally to remove all dead, diseased and damaged growth, then thin densely tangled shoots and shorten any over-long ones that spoil the plant's symmetry. Alternatively, remove all but the strongest shoots, then reduce these by about one-third of their length. This suits many cultivars of American origin that may not adapt well to climates with cool summers and mild, damp winters.

Standard roses

Most standards are top-grafted with buds from large- or cluster-flowered bush roses. In early spring, cut back all shoots by about one-third of their length, to produce a balanced head (see below). If the head is unbalanced, prune the weaker side harder to encourage more vigorous growth. For weeping standards formed from small-flowered ramblers, remove the old, flowered wood when flowers have faded, and leave the growth from the current season intact.

HOW TO PRUNE A MINIATURE ROSE

Before
Miniature roses often produce a mass of twiggy growth, with vigorous over-long shoots arising from the base that spoil the plant's symmetry.

After
All twiggy and damaged wood has been removed, and remaining shoots have been reduced by one-third to one-half of their length.

HOW TO PRUNE A STANDARD ROSE

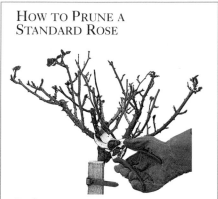

Before
In late autumn or early spring, prune to prevent the plant from becoming too top-heavy and to retain an evenly balanced head.

After
Remove dead, damaged, and crossing stems, then reduce the main shoots to about 8–10in (20–25cm) long. Reduce sideshoots by one-third of their length.

Species, shrub and old garden roses

The majority of old garden and shrub roses, and all of the species, bloom mainly on wood that is two or more years old, and, in addition, they often possess a graceful habit that is easily spoiled by pruning incorrectly. Most will bloom freely for many years, provided that dead, diseased, and damaged wood is removed regularly to keep them healthy. Once mature, however, most benefit from regular renewal pruning.

Prune mature, remontant shrub roses lightly in winter. Cut about one-fifth to one quarter of the oldest flowered stems back to the base to encourage new shoots that will flower in the following summer. Non-remontant roses are pruned in the same way immediately after flowering, unless wanted for their hips. Rugosa, China, and Hybrid musk roses may be given similar, annual renewal pruning.

Gallica roses

These dense, free-branching shrubs flower on sideshoots from two-year-old wood. They often produce a tangle of twiggy shoots that should be thinned regularly during the flowering season to allow good air circulation and reduce the risk of fungal diseases. Prune annually after flowering by reducing the sideshoots and removing dead or diseased wood. Over-long shoots may be cut back by up to one-third if they spoil the overall outline. When mature, cut back a proportion of the oldest flowered wood to the base to encourage vigorous replacement shoots. Gallicas are often used for informal hedging; trim each shrub lightly after flowering to maintain a tidy shape. Follow the natural outline of the plant, and take care not to remove too many sideshoots that will bear the following year's flowers.

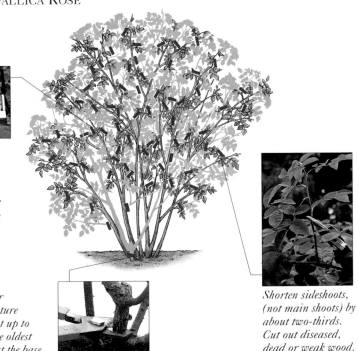

PRUNING A GALLICA ROSE

Throughout the flowering season, thin out twiggy growth regularly and remove spent flowers by cutting back to the shoot they arise from.

Once a year, after flowering, on mature specimens, cut out up to one-quarter of the oldest flowered shoots at the base.

Shorten sideshoots, (not main shoots) by about two-thirds. Cut out diseased, dead or weak wood.

Albas, Provence, Damask, and Moss roses

These roses flower on two-year-old wood; a few Damasks also produce some blooms on the current year's growth in late summer or autumn. Prune after flowering by reducing the main shoots by a quarter to one-third of their length, and sideshoots by about two-thirds. At the end of summer, reduce any over-long whippy shoots by about a third to reduce risk of wind-rock in winter. Mature plants respond well to renewal pruning, as described for Gallicas.

Bourbon and Hybrid Perpetual roses

These are usually remontant, so prune them, and all hybrids derived from *R. rugosa*, in late winter or early spring, using the same technique as described for Hybrid Teas, (p.141), but much more lightly.

Species roses

The species roses flower on two-year-old wood, usually bearing their flowers on short sideshoots all along the length of their arching shoots. They need formative pruning to establish a framework of strong shoots but thereafter need little regular pruning other than the routine removal of dead, diseased, and damaged growth. If they become too dense, or if flowering wood ceases to be productive, they may be renewal pruned after flowering, as described for the non-remontant shrub roses. Very old specimens can be rejuvenated by severe pruning. This requires patience; although hard pruning encourages strong vegetative growth, the new wood will not bloom until its second year. If the bush becomes lopsided, re-shape after flowering and trim back over-long shoots.

PRUNING ALBA, PROVENCE, DAMASK, AND MOSS ROSES

After flowering, reduce sideshoots by two-thirds, and main shoots by one-third to one-quarter.

If necessary, prune again in late summer, after flowering, reducing any over-long shoots by about one-third of their length, to minimize the risk of wind-rock in winter.

Groundcover roses

There are two broad groups of ground-cover roses. The majority are low-growing, spreading, modern shrub roses of dense habit, and these are renewal pruned as for the shrub roses (p.144). A number are creeping, stem-rooting cultivars, like *R.* 'Grouse', whose habit reveals that their parentage involves the rambler *R. wichuraiana*. These need pruning only to restrict growth, and to confine to the space available (see right).

Pegging down roses

This technique was widely used by 19th-century gardeners to create a sheet of bloom over the rose surface, either at ground level, or on a wood and wire frame, about 18in (45cm) high, enclosed by boxwood or lavender hedging. It can be used for increasing flower production on any rose that produces long flexible shoots, but is particularly useful for Bourbon or Hybrid Perpetual roses, which produce whippy shoots that tend to bear flowers at the tips. Pegging down encourages the production of flowering sideshoots in much the same way as for espaliered apples or rambling and climbing roses. In late summer or early

PRUNING GROUNDCOVER ROSES

For groundcover roses of creeping, stem-rooting habit, prune shoots back to well within the intended area of spread, cutting back to an upward-facing bud.

autumn, bend the stems over gently, and peg them down firmly into the ground using wire hoops. Alternatively, tie them onto wires stretched between wooden uprights. Prune the sideshoots back annually to 4–6in (10–15cm); in early spring for remontant roses, or after flowering for non-remontant ones.

PEGGING DOWN

In late summer or autumn, select long flexible shoots and bend them down gently to the horizontal. Prune the soft tips and peg down firmly.

Use sturdy wire hoops to fasten the shoots firmly into the soil.

How to Prune and Train a Climbing Rose

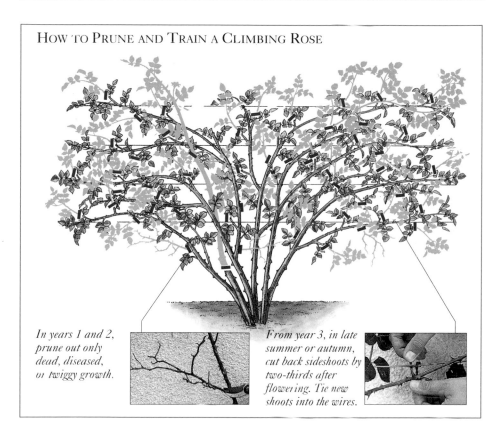

In years 1 and 2, prune out only dead, diseased, or twiggy growth.

From year 3, in late summer or autumn, cut back sideshoots by two-thirds after flowering. Tie new shoots into the wires.

Climbers and ramblers

The difference between climbers and ramblers is a source of much confusion. The diverse heritage of their breeding often muddles the distinction between the two, and some roses are "borderline" cases. The division is rather artificial, but in general, climbers have long, rather stiff stems, are usually remontant, and bear large flowers singly or in small clusters. Climbers of very stiff habit are most easily trained on walls and fences but can be trained on pergolas, pillars, and arches, provided that growth is trained in before it has matured and hardened. Ramblers are usually of more lax growth, tend to produce smaller flowers in large clusters, and are seldom remontant. The long stems are usually more flexible, and new ones are produced more readily from the base

than those of climbers. These flexible stems lend themselves particularly well to training on arches, pergolas, and pillars.

Climbing roses

Unless they have made exceptional growth, climbers should not be pruned in their first or second year except to remove dead, diseased, or weak growth. Never prune climbing sports of bush or shrub roses in the first two years.

Begin training as soon as the new shoots reach the supports. They flower best if trained on horizontal supports, which encourages the production of flowering sideshoots. If space is restricted, training on diagonal wires will have a similar though lesser effect. Most climbers flower well for years with little pruning other than routine removal of dead, diseased, and weak growth. For best results, however, begin regular pruning in the third year, in autumn, after flowering. Prune the main shoots only to tip them back when they outgrow their allotted space. Prune short sideshoots back by about two-thirds, cutting back to an outward-facing bud. Longer sideshoots may be treated as main shoots. Train and tie in all new growth to the support to fill in or extend the framework. If the base of the rose becomes bare, prune one or two of the oldest flowered shoots back to within 12in (30cm) of the base to encourage vigorous new replacement shoots. Water freely the following spring. Repeat this renewal pruning as necessary in subsequent years.

Rambling roses

Like climbing roses, many ramblers flower well for years without formal pruning. They do, however, produce much more growth from the base than climbers. If these shoots are not carefully trained and controlled, they produce a tangled mass of stems that results in poor air circulation, and greater incidence of fungal diseases.

Prune ramblers in summer, after flowering. In the first two years, restrict pruning to cutting back all sideshoots to a vigorous shoot, and removing dead or diseased wood. Train the growing shoots onto wires, tying in as close to the horizontal as possible, to encourage the production of flowering sideshoots along the main stems. In the third and subsequent years, prune out no more than a quarter to one-third of the old, flowered shoots annually, cutting them back to the base with loppers. Leave the most vigorous of the older shoots in place, and fill in the gaps in the framework by tying in the new shoots that have emerged from the base. This may be done in one of two ways. If growth is not too congested, remove old shoots in sections to avoid disturbing or damaging the remaining stems. Where growth is tangled, untie all the shoots from their support, and lay them on the ground before pruning. After thinning, remove unripe wood from the tips of the remaining main shoots, and cut back sideshoots to leave 2–4 healthy buds on each.

How to Prune and Train a Mature Rambling Rose

After year 2, prune in late summer as soon as flowering is over. Cut sideshoots back to 2–4 buds. In year 3, cut out some of the oldest shoots at the base.

Tie in all new shoots into the wires, as close to the horizontal as possible.

PROPAGATION

Most roses, especially those of complex parentage, are propagated commercially by bud-grafting onto specially selected and pre-prepared rootstocks. This technique requires skill but produces vigorous plants quickly, offering economies of time and scale to the commercial producer. For the amateur gardener, propagating by cuttings, seed, layers, or division, produces satisfactory results, but do bear in mind that complex hybrids increased by these methods may lack the vigor of their bud-grafted counterparts.

Hardwood cuttings

Most roses can be propagated by taking hardwood cuttings. This is particularly successful for simple hybrids, or those closely related to species roses, as are many of the ramblers. Most miniature roses root very easily and are propagated commercially in this way. Hybrid Teas and Floribundas of complex parentage root less readily and may take 2–3 years to root, establish, and grow on to sufficient size for planting out. Prepare a cutting bed in late summer, in an open site, preferably with some shade

---

HARDWOOD CUTTINGS

1 *Choose a healthy, well-ripened, pencil-thick shoot that has flowered in summer and is 1–2ft (30–60cm) long. Remove it with an angled cut, just above an outward-facing bud. Remove soft tips and leaves.*

2 *Cut into lengths of 9in (23cm), with an angled cut above the top bud and a straight cut below the bottom bud. Dip in rooting hormone.*

3 *Make planting holes 6in (15cm) deep, 6in (15cm) apart. Trickle a 1in (2.5cm) layer of sharp sand into the bottom.*

4 *Insert the cuttings with the bottom 6in (15cm) buried in the hole. Make sure they touch the bottom. Firm, water, and label.*

5 *A year later, lift each rooted cutting with a hand fork. Plant out into a nursery bed or cold frame to grow on.*

from midday sun. Dig the area, firm, then rake to produce an even surface. Take hardwood cuttings from healthy, well-ripened shoots of the current season's growth in early autumn. Insert them as shown (p.149), or root them in deep pots of light sandy soil, plunged in an open frame outdoors. Check the cuttings regularly, water them in dry periods and, in winter, refirm any that have been lifted by frost. Remove any flower buds that develop during summer. They should be well-rooted by the following autumn. If they are large enough (9in/23cm) tall), they may be transplanted to their permanent position. If not, grow on for another year in pots or nursery beds.

HOW TO LAYER ROSES

Preparing the stem
Make a 1in (2.5cm) slit on the underside of the stem. Dust the cut with rooting hormone, and wedge it open with a matchstick (see inset).

Pegging down
Position the shoot in a slight depression in prepared soil, and peg down with a wire hoop. Cover with soil, firm in, and tie the shoot tip to a short vertical stake.

Semi-ripe cuttings

In areas that experience severe winters, semi-ripe cuttings may be more successful than hardwood cuttings. In summer, after flowering, select mature sideshoots that are still green. Take 6in (15cm) lengths, cutting just above a bud where the shoots are beginning to turn woody, and trim off the soft tips. Prepare the cuttings about 4in (10cm) long, remove the thorns and lowest leaves, and treat the base with rooting hormone. Insert them to two-thirds of their length in deep pots containing a mix of equal parts peat and sharp sand. Firm and water in, then cover the pots with a plastic bag supported by stakes or wire hoops, or put them in a propagator, to prevent them from drying out. Keep them moist in a cool, frost-free place, and shade from hot sun. Check regularly and remove any fallen leaves. In spring, plant the rooted cuttings in a nursery bed.

Layering roses

Any rose with shoots that are sufficiently long and flexible to be bent over and pegged down into the ground may be propagated by simple layering. This is an ideal method for increasing rambling and climbing roses and many shrub roses, such as the Bourbons, Damasks, Provence, and most Albas and species roses. Many groundcover roses can also be layered, and some, such as R. 'Grouse', produce natural layers by rooting where they touch the soil.

In summer, after flowering, select a shoot of healthy, mature wood. Create a clear length of stem by removing some of the leaves. Make a 1in (2.5cm) slit on the lower side of the stem, dust with rooting hormone, and wedge it open with a spent matchstick. Incorporate some peat into the ground where the shoot is to be layered, then peg it firmly into a small depression in the soil, using a wire hoop. Cover with soil, firm in, and tie the shoot tip to a short, vertical cane. Separate the rooted layer from the parent plant the following spring.

Propagating roses from seed

Species roses, unlike cultivars, come true from seed, although their offspring may show a certain amount of natural variation. A few seed merchants offer seed, but seeds are easily extracted from the ripe hips of mature roses in your own garden.

In the autumn, extract the seeds from plump, ripe hips and stratify them by placing them in a plastic bag or cup of moist seed soil mix or perlite, which should be stored in the refrigerator at about 34–41°F (1–5°C) for 3–6 weeks. Sow into individual pots or in seed trays, spacing at about 2in (5cm) apart. Cover

RAISING ROSES FROM SEED

1 *Slit open a ripe hip (see inset) with a sharp knife. Remove the seeds individually with the point of the knife blade. Avoid skin contact; seeds are clothed in irritant hairs.*

2 *Place the seed in a plastic bag of moist soilless seed mix or perlite and keep it at room temperature for 2–3 days. Then store in a refrigerator for 3–6 weeks, at a temperature of 34–41°F (1–5°C).*

3 *Sow the seed singly into commercial seed mix or a mix of equal parts of peat and sand. Cover the seeds to their own depth with a layer of fine grit and place in a cold frame. Label the pots clearly.*

4 *When the first pair of true leaves emerges, prick the seedlings out singly into a 2in (5cm) pot filled with a soil-based potting mix. Grow on, and repot as necessary until large enough to plant out.*

PROPAGATING ROSES BY DIVISION

1 *In late autumn or early spring, select a well-developed sucker. Scrape away the soil to expose its base, then sever it from the parent with as many roots as possible.*

2 *Prepare a hole, wide and deep enough to accommodate the roots. Plant the sucker immediately, firm, and water in (see inset). Trim the shoots back to 9–12in (23–30cm).*

the seeds to their own depth with sharp sand or grit. Place in a cold frame, and cover with fine mesh wire to protect against mice. Germination may be erratic and will take between 12–24 months, so do not discard the containers if nothing germinates in the first spring.

Prick out seedlings into individual containers as soon as the first pair of true rose leaves has developed. The seed leaves are oval and quite unlike typical rose leaves. Handle the seedlings only by their leaves, since both the stem and root are fragile and easily damaged. Grow the young seedlings in a cold frame until they have become well established in their pots, then harden off gradually. Once acclimatized, grow on in the open, repotting as necessary until they are large enough to be planted out.

New rose cultivars are grown from seed that results from the hand pollination of selected seed parents by selected pollen parents. The aim is to produce offspring that inherit the best characteristics of both parents, although the chances of producing a high-quality

cultivar with distinct characteristics are relatively small. When a good new rose is eventually selected from thousands of seedlings, it is budded onto seedling rootstocks, and then subjected to trials for several years before being introduced to the commercial market.

Propagating roses by division

If a rose is grown on its own roots, taking rooted suckers and growing them on is an easy method of propagation. Some species grown from seed, and others grown from cuttings, sucker naturally. Cultivars of *R. pimpinellifolia*, *R. rugosa*, and some Gallicas sucker freely and are readily increased this way. In the dormant season, separate rooted suckers from the parent and plant them out either in a nursery bed or, if large enough, transfer directly to their flowering site. Occasionally, deep planting of budded cultivars induces the cultivar shoots to produce roots, and these rooted shoots may be propagated in the same way as rooted suckers, if removed very carefully from the parent.

Roses for display and exhibition

Many roses in this book are described as "suitable for exhibition," and it can be very satisfying to enter your roses in a local, or even a regional show. High levels of competition demand impeccable standards of cultivation, and rules for showing are detailed and strict. Exhibitors grow several bushes of the same cultivar to ensure a wide choice of blooms. The bushes are severely pruned to produce a limited number of shoots with only 8–9 perfect blooms in a season. They also need additional fertilizer and good pest and disease control. Roses are often disbudded to produce exhibition-quality blooms. Having produced perfect blooms, timing is critical when exhibiting them. Generally, a Hybrid Tea rose should be three-quarters open at the moment of judging, while for Floribundas, the clusters must have blooms in a cycle of openness, although the stamens should not have blackened. To learn more about growing and exhibiting roses, join your local or national rose society to enjoy access to a wealth of experience and knowledge of rose-growing.

CHINESE HATS

Some blooms are are easily damaged by rain, and show rules permit the use of individual bloom protectors in the form of a plastic cone, or "Chinese hat." They are easier to use on single blooms of Hybrid Tea roses than on the large clusters of Floribundas. Insert a stake with a "Chinese hat" by the rose stem and tie the stem in to the stake.

DISBUDDING ROSES

Hybrid Tea roses
As soon as they are large enough to handle, pinch out all sidebuds, leaving the main central bud to grow on.

Floribunda Roses
Pinch out the young central bud of each smaller spray in the cluster if you want the remaining flowers all open at the same time.

GLOSSARY OF TERMS

Italicized words have their own entry.

ACID (of soil). With a *pH* value of less than 7, or lacking in lime; see also *alkaline* and *neutral*.

ALKALINE (of soil). With a pH value of more than 7, or lime-rich; see also *acid* and *neutral*.

ANTHER. The part of a *stamen* that produces pollen.

AXIL. The angle between a leaf and stem where an axillary bud develops.

BACKFILL. To fill in a planting hole around a plant's roots with a soil mix.

BALLED. Of a flower that does not open properly and rots when still in bud.

BARE-ROOT. Of plants sold with their roots bare of soil

BUD. A rudimentary or condensed shoot containing an embryonic leaf, leaf cluster, or flower.

BUSH. A small *shrub*.

CALYX. The outer part of a flower, usually small and green but in some genera it may be showy and brightly colored; it is formed from the sepals and encloses the petals in a bud.

CLIMBER. A plant that climbs using other plants or objects as support.

CROCKS. Broken pieces of clay pot, used to cover drainage holes of pots in order to provide free drainage and air circulation to the root system and to stop the growing medium from escaping, or blocking, the holes.

CULTIVAR. A contraction of "cultivated variety" ("cv"); a group (or one among such a group) of cultivated plants clearly distinguished by one or more characteristics and which retains these characteristics when propagated.

DEADHEADING. The removal of spent flowers or *flower heads*.

DIEBACK. The death of tips or shoots due to damage or disease.

DISBUDDING. The removal of surplus buds to encourage production of high-quality blooms.

DIVISION. A method of propagation by which a plant is divided into separate parts during dormancy. See *Guide to Rose Care*, pp.152.

DORMANCY. The state of temporary cessation of growth and slowing down of other activities in whole plants, usually during winter.

ESPALIER. A plant trained with the main stem vertical and (usually) three or more tiers of branches horizontally placed on either side in a single plane.

EVERGREEN. Retaining its leaves all year round, although losing some older leaves regularly throughout the year. Semi-evergreen plants retain only some leaves or lose older leaves only when new growth is produced.

FAMILY. A category in plant classification, a grouping together of related *genera*, for example, the family Rosaceae includes the genera *Rosa, Sorbus, Rubus, Prunus*, and *Pyracantha*.

FLOWER. The part of the plant containing the reproductive organs, usually surrounded by *sepals* and *petals*. For the different types of rose flowers see *Roses in the Garden*, p.9.

FRAMEWORK. The permanent branch structure of a tree or shrub; the main branches that determine its ultimate shape.

FRIABLE. Soil of a crumbly texture, able to be worked easily.

GENUS (pl. genera). A category in plant classification, consisting of a group of related *species*.

GLAUCOUS. Blue-green, blue-gray, or white with a bluish, grayish or whitish bloom.

GLOBOSE. Spherical.

GRAFTING. Method of propagation by which an artificial union is made between a shoot or bud of one plant and the rootstock of another so that they eventually function as one plant.

GRAFT UNION. The point at which the *scion* and *rootstock* are joined.

GROUNDCOVER. Usually low-growing plants that quickly cover the soil surface and suppress weeds.

HABIT. The characteristic growth or general appearance of a plant.

HARDWOOD CUTTING. A method of propagation by which a cutting is taken from mature wood at the end of the growing season. See *Guide to Rose Care*, p.149.

HEEL. The small portion of old wood that is retained at the base of a cutting when it is removed from the stem.

HUMUS. The organic residue of decayed vegetable matter in soil. Also often used to describe partly decayed matter such as leaf mold or compost.

HYBRID. The offspring of genetically different parents, usually produced accidentally or artificially in cultivation, but occasionally arising in the wild.

INCURVED. Applied to *petals* and *florets* that curve inward to form a compact, rounded shape.

LATERAL. A side growth that arises from a shoot or root.

LAYERING. A method of propagation by which a stem is induced to root by being pegged down to the soil while still attached to the parent plant. See *Guide to Rose Care*, p.150.

LEAFLET. A subdivision of a compound leaf.

MICROCLIMATE. A small, local climate within a larger climate area, such as a greenhouse or a protected area of a garden.

MULCH. A layer of *organic* matter applied to the soil over or around a plant to conserve moisture, protect the roots from frost, reduce the growth of weeds, and enrich the soil.

NEUTRAL (of soil). With a pH value of 7, the point at which soil is neither acid nor alkaline.

NON-REMONTANT. Flowering only once in a single flush. (Cf. *Remontant.*)

NUTRIENTS. Minerals (mineral ions) used to develop proteins and other compounds required for plant growth.

ORGANIC. 1. Compounds containing carbon derived from decomposed plant or animal organisms. 2. Used loosely of mulches, soil mixes, etc. derived from plant materials.

PETAL. One portion of the often bright and colored part of the *corolla*.

PETIOLE. The stalk of a leaf.

pH. A measure of alkalinity or acidity, used horticulturally to refer to soils. The scale measures from 1 to 14; pH7 is neutral, above 7 is *alkaline*, and below 7 *acid*.

PROPAGATOR. A structure that provides a humid atmosphere for seedlings, cuttings, or other plants being propagated.

RAMBLER. A large-growing, once-blooming rose, usually bearing large clusters of smallish flowers.

REMONTANT. Of a plant that flowers more than once during the growing season.

RENEWAL PRUNING. A system in which the *laterals* are constantly cut back to be replaced by young laterals stimulated by pruning.

REVERT. To return to an original state, as when plain green leaves are produced on a variegated plant.

ROOT. The part of a plant, normally underground, that functions as an anchorage and through which nutrients are absorbed.

ROOT BALL. The roots and accompanying soil or soil mix visible when a plant is removed from a container.

ROOTSTOCK. A plant used to provide the root system for a *grafted* plant.

SCION. A *shoot* or *bud* cut from one plant to *graft* onto a *rootstock* (stock) of another.

SEEDLING. A young plant that has developed from a seed.

SEPAL. Part of a *calyx*. Though usually green and insignificant, they may sometimes be showy.

SHOOT. A branch, stem, or twig.

SHRUB. A *woody*-stemmed plant, usually branching from or near the base.

SIDESHOOT. A stem that arises from the side of a main *shoot*.

SNAG. A short stub or frayed end left after inexpert pruning.

SPECIES. A category in plant classification, the rank below *genus*, containing related, individual plants.

SPECIMEN PLANT. A striking plant, usually a tree or shrub in prime condition, grown where it can be seen clearly.

SPENT (of flowers). Dying or dead.

SPORT. A mutation, caused by an induced or spontaneous genetic change, which may produce shoots with different characteristics, or flowers of a different color from the parent plant.

SPRAY. A group of *flowers* on a single, branching stem.

STAMEN. The male floral organ, bearing an *anther* that produces pollen.

STANDARD. A plant grafted on a type of rootstock that provides a clear length of stem below the branches, 80cm–1.2m (2½–4ft) for most roses.

STIGMA. The area of the female part of the flower which receives pollen.

STYLE. The part of the flower on which the *stigma* is carried.

SUCKER. 1. A shoot that arises below ground from a plant's roots or underground stem. 2) on *grafted* plants, a sucker is any shoot that originates below the *graft union*.

TRANSLOCATED (of dissolved *nutrients* or weedkillers). Moving within the vascular system (conducting tissues) of a plant.

TRUSS. A compact cluster of fruits or flowers, often large and showy.

VARIETY. Botanically, a naturally occurring variant (varietas – var.) of a wild *species*.

VEGETATIVE GROWTH. Non-flowering, usually leafy growth.

WHIP. A young seedling or grafted tree without lateral branches.

UNDERPLANTING. Low-growing plants planted beneath larger plants.

WINDROCK. The destabilizing of a plant's roots by winds.

WOODY. With branches of hard, woody fibers, that persist, unlike soft-stemmed herbaceous plants. A semi-woody stem contains some softer tissue and may be only partially persistent.

INDEX

All roses belong to the genus *Rosa*. All species of *Rosa* are given in italics; cultivars are in Roman type with single quotes.

ACKNOWLEDGMENTS

Key. t=top, b=bottom; r right; l=left

The publishers would like to thank the following for their kind permission to reproduce the photographs:

Peter Beales 19bl, 46tl, 118br
Neil Campbell-Sharp 83bl
Michael Gibson 72tr
Derek Gould 17tl, 72l
R.Harkness & Co Ltd. 19tl, 28bl, 38bl, 73bl, 102tr
P. Harkness 19tr
Andrew Lawson 87br, 111tl, 114l
Vincent Page 30tr, 65tr, 80tl, 96bl
Photos Horticultural Photo Library 24br, 112tr, 122tr, 128l
Harry Smith Collection 28tr, 39br, 46bl, 54bl, 77br, 79r, 118bl, 121tl, 121bl, 122br, 123tl, 131bl
Alistair Urquhart 70br
Chris Warner 112bl
Wheatcroft Ltd 95bl

Special photography: Howard Rice, Clive Boursnall, Eric Crichton,
John Glover, Jerry Harpur, Andrew Lawson, Andrew de Lory

Special thanks for help with photography The Royal National Rose Society, St. Albans, Herts

Abbreviations			
C	centrigrade	in	inch, inches
cm	centimeter	m	meter
cv.	cultivar	mm	millimeter
F	Fahrenheit	oz	ounce
f.	forma	sp.	species
ft	foot, feet	subsp.	subspecies
g	gram	var.	variant

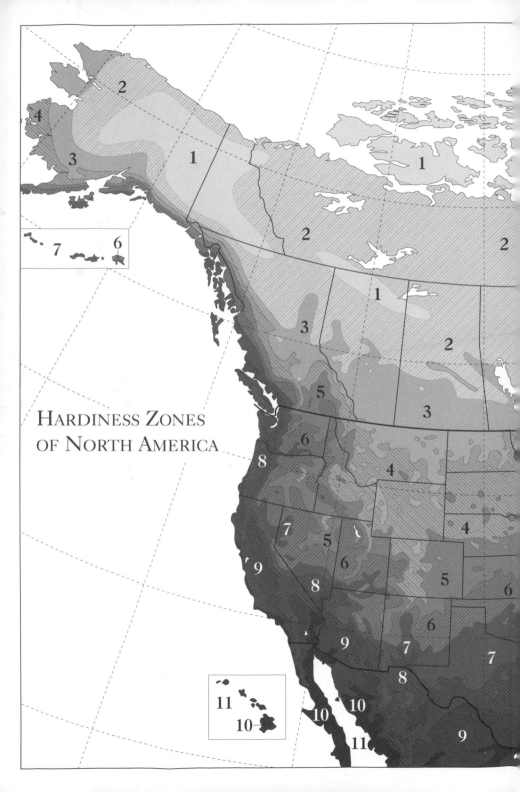

HARDINESS ZONES
OF NORTH AMERICA